ILLUSTRATED HISTORY OF
WORLD WAR I

Daddy, what did YOU do in the Great War?

ADRIAN GILBERT

ILLUSTRATED HISTORY OF
WORLD
WAR I

Portland House
A Division of Crown Publishers, Inc.
A Bison Book

This 1988 edition published by
Portland House, distributed by
Crown Publishers, Inc.
225 Park Avenue South
New York, NY 10003

Produced by
Bison Books Corp.
15 Sherwood Place
Greenwich, CT 06830
USA

Printed in Italy

Library of Congress Cataloging-in-Publication Data
Gilbert, Adrian.
Illustrated History of World War I/by Adrian Gilbert.
p.   cm.
ISBN 0-517-65843-7
1. World War, 1914-1918   I. Title
D521.G55 1988
940.3— dc19   87-34784
        CIP

PAGE 1: *Two contrasting British views of the war – a
recruiting poster cleverly designed to appeal to a man's
patriotic and masculine pride, and an example of the real
thing – a shell-shocked young soldier in the trenches.*

PAGES 2-3: *A painting by the renowned war artist Christopher
Nevinson depicting the horrors of the battlefield.*

PAGES 4-5: *The scream of an incoming German shell sends an
American patrol diving for cover.*

Contents

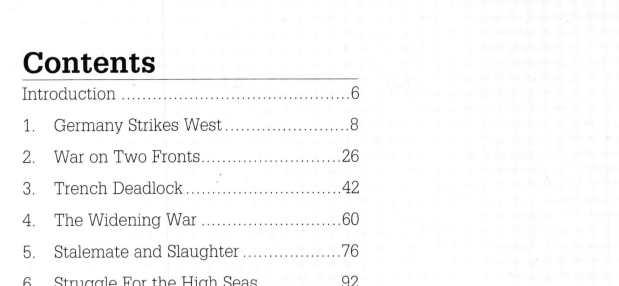

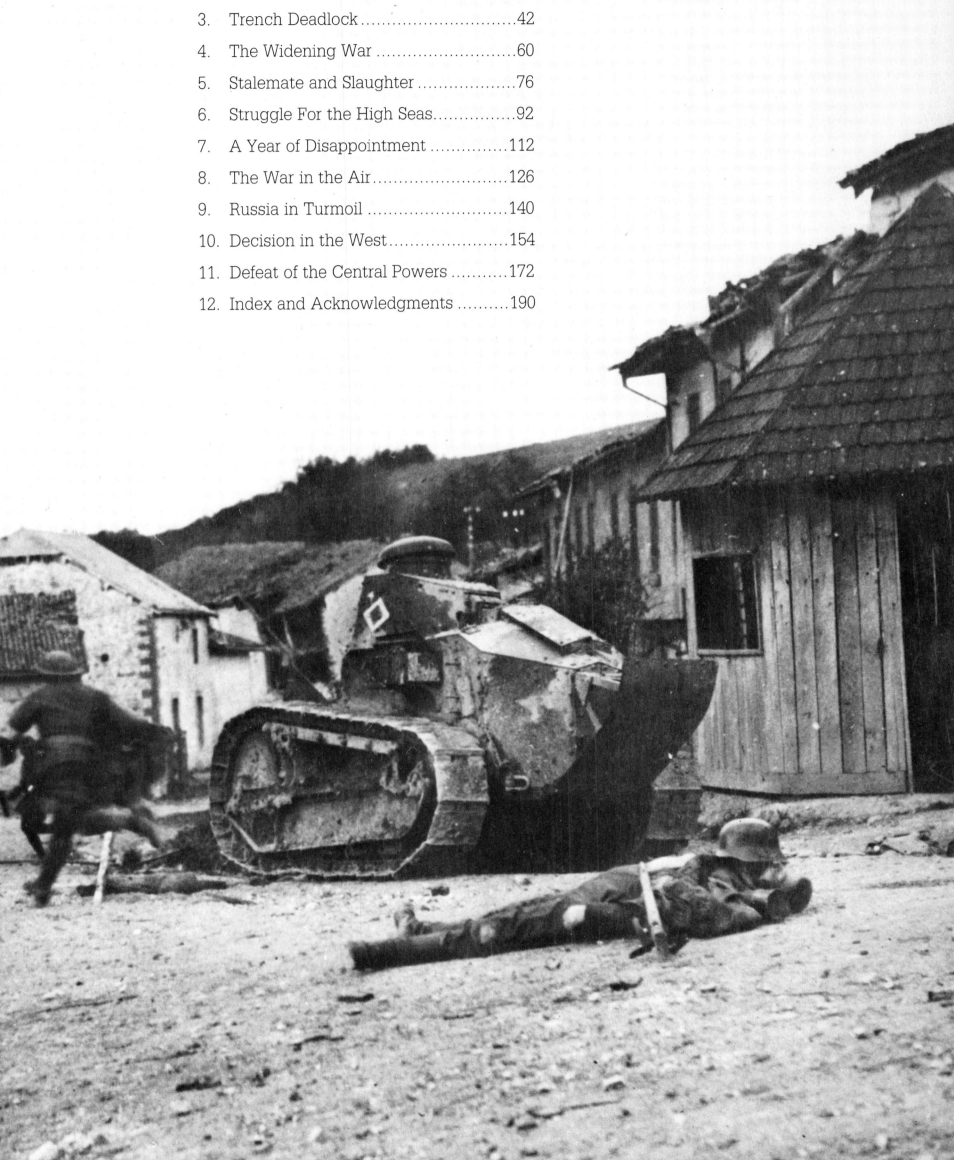

On 28 June 1914 a young Serbian nationalist, Gavrilo Princip, pushed his way through the crowds lining the streets of the Bosnian city of Sarajevo and fired three shots into the body of Archduke Franz Ferdinand, mortally wounding the heir to the Austro-Hungarian Empire. To the horrified onlookers the enormity of the act was obvious, but few then could have foreseen that this particular Balkan assassination would lead directly and inexorably to a global war of almost indescribable destruction. The adjectives 'Great' and 'World' were to be no exaggeration – this conflict was the first modern industrial war, the consequences of which are still with us today.

The driving force which shaped the economic expansion of Europe in the nineteenth century was, quite simply, the search for markets in which to sell the mass-produced output of the industrial revolution. By 1914, however, the search was becoming increasingly competitive and the economic rivalry between European powers had acquired an edge unknown in the previous century. The motivation behind the acquisition of the great colonial empires had largely been the desire for economic expansion and to safeguard national markets, but by 1914 there was little left of the world to be colonized and disputes between the European states over territorial ownership in Africa and Asia became markedly more frequent.

The overall increase in superpower rivalry was worsened by Germany's position within this inner circle. In 1914, by almost any economic or military yardstick, Germany was the most powerful nation in Europe, but she had only achieved unification in 1871 and, as a newcomer to the world stage, had lost out in the great surge of empire building in the nineteenth century. Britain and France had been the main beneficiaries of colonialism and Germany felt acute frustration at being 'cheated' out of her just rewards.

A young, aggressive nation, the Germany of Kaiser Wilhelm II sat uneasily at the high table of the great powers. Germany's international frustration was only one expression of the profound instability within the nation as a whole. Although Germany was in the vanguard of economic progress, her system of government remained distinctly feudal in character. The German parliament (Reichstag) was hardly comparable to its French and British equivalents – when the crunch came power in Germany lay in the hands of the generals. Alongside the Army chiefs was the Kaiser, another element contributing to the fateful instability of 1914 Germany. Vain, weak and possessed of a deep-seated inferiority complex, Wilhelm represented all that was bad in Germany. And like his ostensible subordinates in the Army, the Kaiser had little understanding of international politics: diplomacy was dispensed with in favor of crude confrontational tactics which at times degenerated into outright intimidation, and his foreign ministry displayed a cynical disregard for international commitments made by the government.

Germany's main ally, Austria-Hungary, was racked with an instability of a very different sort. Whereas Germany was a single, cohesive national state, the Austro-Hungarian Empire was an aggregate of Slavic states ruled by Teutonic Austria and Magyar Hungary. Yet the nineteenth century was the age of the nation state. In the course of the century nationalism had traveled steadily eastward from its birthplace in France, so that by 1900 the Austro-Hungarian Empire was being torn apart at the seams. The decline of the other Balkan empire, Turkey, had led to the emergence of the independent states of Serbia, Bulgaria, Rumania, Albania and Greece.

The old animosity between Teutons and Slavs was focused on the deteriorating relationship between Austria and Serbia, the former accusing the latter of supporting terrorist activity by Slav nationalists within the empire. There was some truth in these accusations and to the

ABOVE: *A few moments after the fatal deed, the young Serbian assassin Gavrilo Princip (center) is led away by horrified officials, 28 June 1914.*

LEFT: *Always a faintly ludicrous figure, Kaiser Wilhelm II of Germany accentuates this 'failing' by his determinedly martial pose and choice of headgear.*

Austrians the assassination of Franz Ferdinand was the final provocation in a series of perceived humiliations inflicted upon them by Serbia. That Austria-Hungary should have taken its retribution to the point of declaring war on Serbia was extreme but not a total surprise. The question then arises of why a local dispute between two Balkan states should lead to a world war within a matter of weeks? The answer lay in the nature of the system of alliances which bound and divided Europe into two separate armed camps.

The struggle for the domination of central Europe had been won decisively by Germany in wars against Denmark, Austria and France in the nineteenth century. After the Franco-Prussian War (1870-71) the German Chancellor, Count Otto von Bismarck, had followed up the military victories with a series of treaties designed to maintain Germany's ascendent position in Europe. When,

ABOVE: *Count Alfred von Schlieffen, Chief of the German General Staff 1891-1905. His plan ensured that any forthcoming war would become a global conflict. An able strategist, Schlieffen's political naivety led to disaster for Germany.*

BELOW: *Emperor Franz Joseph of Austria-Hungary. Both he and his political system were anachronisms by the early twentieth century.*

RIGHT: *A rather inept German caricature of Sir Edward Grey, the British Foreign Secretary during the July-August crisis of 1914. Despite the 'two faces' Grey was no enthusiast for war; only Germany's invasion of Belgium forced Britain to declare war.*

however, Wilhelm II came to the throne and removed Bismarck in 1889, the system fell apart. Russia, previously bound by a treaty of friendship to Germany, moved toward an arrangement with France, especially when Germany and Austria-Hungary drew closer together. Thus Germany had potential enemies to both west and east. Traditionally, Britain remained outside any direct involvement in such international treaty obligations, although the emergence of Germany as an aggressive economic rival began to cause concern. But it was Germany's decision to challenge Britain's position as the premier naval power (through the building of her own modern battle fleet) which pushed Britain into an alliance (albeit informal) with France. These treaties were intended to be essentially defensive in character, but a series of international incidents – Morocco (1905), Bosnia (1908-09) and Agadir (1911) – lessened international trust and generally increased tension.

As the European powers were becoming increasingly polarized into two rival camps, war plans were drawn up to cover the possibility – or probability – of outright conflict. The strategic situation was geographically determined: Germany and Austria-Hungary held the center, 'surrounded' by France and Russia, while Britain occupied a peripheral position in the scheme of things. Britain's military and naval potential was dismissed by both her enemy (Germany) and ally (France).

While the Central Powers of Germany and Austria-Hungary had the advantage of operating on interior lines, Germany was faced with the prospect of war on two fronts and her strategic plans reflected this. The Chief of the German General Staff during the key years of 1891-1905 was Count Alfred von Schlieffen. He proposed to strike a swift and massive blow against France – sufficient to knock her out of the war – and subsequently turn eastward to deal with Russia. Schlieffen's plan was a gambler's throw, dependent on the speed of German mobilization, the completeness of the victory over France and the slowness of Russia's mobilization plans. But in addition to overcoming these 'variables,' Schlieffen's plan was made infamously grotesque by its strategic inflexibility: no matter where the threat or danger originated, Germany must immediately invade France. At the end of July 1914 doubts were expressed as to the advisability of

attacking in the West when the source of conflict lay in the Balkans, but the German General Staff crushed all dissent with the blanket reply that to change the rail schedules would throw the German Army into complete disarray. Once committed, there could be no going back.

This was the first great act of madness of World War I: strategy was subordinated to railway timetables. In addition, although of little interest to Schlieffen and his planners, the invasion of France involved the violation of Belgian neutrality. Prussia had been a cosignatory to Belgian neutrality; and so had Britain.

Sure in the knowledge of German support, Austria-Hungary overrode Serbia's diplomatic attempts to prevent conflict and declared war against the Balkan kingdom on 28 July 1914. Russia then mobilized her frontier forces. On 1 August Germany declared war against Russia and two days later followed this up with the declaration of war against France. On 3 August, German troops invaded Belgium and on the following day – in order to fulfill her guarantee of Belgian neutrality – Britain declared war on Germany.

The last great European war had ended in 1815, and a century later there was much debate as to what exact form the coming war would take. Many military commentators and soldiers expected a short war, complete with one or two decisive battles. The Franco-Prussian War and the recent conflict between Russia and Japan (1904-05) were considered to be the most likely historical precedents, although in fact the American Civil War (1861-65) was to prove the most appropriate model. Among other things, the conduct of the American war provided two factors which were to give World War I its particularly destructive character.

Firstly, until the advent of the nation state armies had been small professional entities, distinct from society as a whole, but the vast citizen armies which followed the French Revolution changed all that. An individual had rights but he also had responsibilities, and one of them was to bear arms in the defense of his country. The concept of the 'nation-in-arms' was not uncommon in late nineteenth century Europe and (with the exception of Britain) universal conscription was standard practice. As populations expanded, so too did the size of armies. Although there were exceptions, the trend during the nineteenth century was one of improvement in the organization of the state. Accordingly, the empires, kingdoms and republics of Europe were capable of fielding armies numbering millions of men for long periods of time. Such an extended, unproductive use of manpower would have been unthinkable in a pre-industrial economy, but this transition was one of the products of the second key factor, the industrial revolution itself. In addition, the industrial revolution provided the new armies with the equipment and weapons of mass destruction. Technological progress went hand in hand with industrial development and in the two decades leading up to the outbreak of war in 1914 there was a genuine technological revolution which was to have a profound influence on World War I battlefields. New weapons in the air and under the sea joined the existing though vastly improved weapons on land.

The enormous casualties of World War I have been unfairly laid at the door of generals accused of being incompetent butchers who did nothing more than lead their men to slaughter on the wire of No Man's Land. Although the war did indeed reveal many commanders as hopelessly out of their depth, the significant fact was that this conflict was the first modern industrial war. Only when the resolution of the politicians and soldiers to gain outright victory is set against the sheer size of the armies involved and the employment of such destructive weapons can the character of World War I be appreciated.

CHAPTER ONE

GERMANY STRIKES WEST

Once the declarations of war had taken effect, the diplomats and politicians gave way to the generals who commenced the task of deploying their vast armies. The mobilization plans of both Germany and France proceeded smoothly. Ever since the Franco-Prussian War of 1870-71, the Germans had proved themselves masters in the applied science of moving large bodies of troops, and the national railway system had been developed largely to serve the Army's requirements for the rapid transit of men across Germany toward the frontiers in the East and West. More surprising was the success of the French mobilization. Desertions were minimal and the railway system worked effectively, so that for the period from 2 to 18 August some 7000 trains transported 3,781,000 men across France to their respective depots and concentration points. Similarly, prompt mobilization by the Belgians ensured that their frontier garrisons were well up to strength, while from Britain the main body of an expeditionary force (four infantry and one cavalry division) had crossed the English Channel, in secrecy, by 17 August.

The German General Staff had staked everything on a swift and resounding victory against France and accordingly deployed the bulk of the German Army in the West. Some 1,485,000 men, organized into seven armies, were in position along Germany's western frontier by the beginning of August. According to the directives of the Schlieffen Plan the Sixth and Seventh Armies at the southern end of the German line would act in a defensive role, while the other five armies would advance through Luxembourg and southern Belgium, thereby outflanking the French armies, the bulk of which were anyway deployed against the German frontier to the south.

The most northerly German force, the 320,000-strong First Army under General Alexander von Kluck, was called upon to perform the most difficult part of the plan. Acting as the open right flank of the German advance it would have to march considerably farther than any other army, wheeling across Belgium and northern France to

PREVIOUS PAGES: *The key instrument of the Schlieffen Plan – columns of German troops advance westward to outflank and overwhelm the French. Despite the weight of their equipment (at least 60lb), the German infantry maintained the most punishing marching schedules throughout the hot August of 1914.*

LEFT: *General Alexander von Kluck, commander of the German First Army which acted as the extreme right wing of the advance through Belgium.*

RIGHT: *The classic recruiting poster by Alfred Leete of Kitchener's imperious demand for volunteers. Newly appointed as Secretary of State for War, Kitchener was one of the few leaders who realized that the conflict would not be over by Christmas but would involve the mobilization of the entire country.*

BELOW: *German troops pose in jubilant mood on one of the many trains heading for the Belgian and French borders. The German rail system had been designed for the rapid transit of troops to the front.*

encircle the enemy forces. A hard-driving general. Kluck was well chosen for his task and during the campaign he forced his men to perform extraordinary feats of marching. Stretching southward from the First Army were the Second Army (General Karl von Bülow, 260,000 men), Third Army (General Max von Hausen, 180,000 men), Fourth Army (General Albrecht, 180,000 men) and Fifth Army (Crown Prince Wilhelm, 200,000 men). Their combined weight of over one million men would be the hammer to smash the French Army.

In overall command of the German Army during this daring enterprise was the Chief of the General Staff, Colonel General Helmut von Moltke. Indecisive and temperamental, however, Moltke was poorly suited for such a responsibility: not only had he tampered with Schlieffen's master plan – reducing the strength of the northern wing through a more even distribution of forces along the entire front – but he was also to find himself losing control of his forces once the great advance got underway. Even if the Schlieffen Plan was overambitious (given the relative paucity of the forces at Moltke's disposal), it was nonetheless an imaginative attempt to solve Germany's two-front strategic dilemma.

France's grand design to secure victory went under the name of Plan XVII and consisted of a major advance into Lorraine supported by a subsidiary offensive through Alsace. Devoid of real strategic thought, Plan XVII relied on the (supposed) inherent superiority of the offensive. During the years leading up to the outbreak of war, France's military theorists had reduced strategy to the simple transportation of the Army to the battlefield. Once in the realm of tactics, French *élan* and *cran* (grit) would carry all before it. Thus, the strategic ineptitude of Plan XVII was compounded by the unwarranted faith the French Army placed in offensive action as a battle-winning device. The stark defensive realities that machine guns, magazine rifles and quick-firing artillery imposed upon the battlefield were rejected for the Napoleonic fantasy of victorious columns charging with bayonets fixed. The battles of 1914 were to produce a French Army casualty rate higher than at any other time in the war, greater even than those suffered in the offensives in Champagne and Artois in 1915 and Verdun and the Somme in 1916. And in the casualty lists of 1914 were some of the finest soldiers of the French Army. Their loss would be keenly felt.

The armies of Germany and France were broadly similar in organization and equipment. The bulk of each army was made up of infrantrymen armed with magazine-loaded, bolt-action rifles, capable of rapid and accurate fire up to a range of over half a mile. Machine guns had been found effective in the colonial wars of the nineteenth century and more recently in the Russo-Japanese War of 1904-05. A modest provision of two such weapons per battalion was common practice in 1914. Their importance was not fully realized before the onset of hostilities but, once their real worth was appreciated, they were ordered in vast quantities to defend the extensive trenches of the Western Front.

Similarly, the effect of artillery as the decisive arm was not properly understood in 1914, except perhaps by the German Army which was well equipped with large numbers of howitzers whose ability to fire large-caliber, high-explosive shells at a high trajectory was invaluable against fortresses and in trench warfare. The French relied heavily on the 75mm field gun, a weapon capable of an extraordinary rate of fire – 20 rounds per minute – but far less effective than large-caliber howitzers when used against well-entrenched troops. Considerable numbers of horsemen were still employed by all the armies and although there was much talk of battlefield charges their main function was one of forward reconnaissance for the infantry.

In terms of training the German Army was superior to its French opponent. Of special importance was the quality of the German NCOs, who were not only reliable but also capable of taking the initiative in most tactical situations. The French placed far too much emphasis on high morale to overcome limitations in tactical skill. The small British Army, by comparison, was exceptionally well-trained, with an emphasis on musketry skills which would astound the Germans. The Belgian Army was similarly small and undergoing a thorough reorganization in 1914; it would have little chance of holding the well-oiled German war machine once the fighting started.

Early on the morning of 4 August 1914 advance elements of the German Army crossed the border into neutral Belgium. Although little interference was expected from the Belgian Army (117,000 men under the command of King Albert), the fortresses of Liège and Namur were potential obstacles to the easy transit of German forces through the country. Liège, astride the main route into Belgium, was a special problem for which the German planners had made special provision: Skoda 30.5cm and Krupp 42cm super-heavy howitzers reduced the steel and concrete fortifications to rubble in just over a week (8-16 August). Kluck's troops marched into Brussels on the 20th while the remainder of the Belgian Army retired northward to the safety of Antwerp. On the 21st, Bülow's Second Army began its investment of Namur.

LEFT: A few of the hundreds of thousands of volunteers who answered Kitchener's call – men queue patiently outside the Whitehall recruiting office in 1914.

BELOW LEFT: A German 21cm howitzer is brought up into position. The appropriate provision of heavy artillery within the German Army was an important factor in the swift advance through Belgium.

French Infantry in Action: 1914

The famous French poet Charles Peguy was an infantry officer involved in the confusing series of actions which constituted the Battle of the Frontiers. This account of his death under fire by the writer Victor Boudon reveals the fatal consequences of French enthusiasm for the 'spirit of the offensive':

> Climbing the bank, rifle in hand, bent almost double to offer the smallest possible target, tripping over beets and clods of earth, we advanced to the assault . . . A rush, and then a second carried us 200 yards forward. For the moment to go forward, in a single wave without supports, over ground where the forward slope and our conspicuous uniforms made us magnificent targets, with only 150 rounds per man and no chance of more, was madness, a certain and complete massacre. Not a dozen of us would get there.
> 'Down,' yelled Peguy. 'Independent fire.' But himself, he remained stand-

ing, his glasses in his hand, directing our fire, heroic in this hell . . . We fired like madmen, blackened with powder, the rifles scorching our fingers, and between rounds thrusting our hands into the earth to fling up a miserable shelter. On all sides, cries, screams, groans. How many dead? We could no longer count . . .

Peguy remained standing in spite of our shouts of 'Lie down.' He drew himself up as if in challenge to the storm of bullets, as it were to summon the death he had glorified in his verse. At that moment a bullet pierced his forehead. He fell on the hillside without a cry, having seen at last clearly that ultimate vision of the longed-for victory. When, some yards further on, frantically leaping forward, I glanced behind me, I saw stretched on the hot dusty earth, among the broad green leaves, a black and scarlet stain in the midst of so many others, the body of our beloved lieutenant.

French infantry move past a barbed-wire obstacle.

LEFT: *A sentimental German poster depicting one of the millions of farewells of August 1914 that preceded the advance into battle.*

FAR RIGHT: *A painting depicting General Galliéni in the typically dramatized style of military portraiture – he is studying a map of the battlefield and behind him staff officers discuss the situation. Alongside them is one of the famous French 75mm artillery pieces. In the background the battle rages. As Military Governor of Paris, Galliéni was to play a crucial role in the great French counterattack that began the Battle of the Marne.*

RIGHT: *French troops march through a village on their way to take part in the 'Battle of the Frontiers.'*

BELOW RIGHT: *The Schlieffen Plan in actuality, revealing the German advance through Belgium and the movement of Kluck's army east of Paris.*

The speed of the German advance through Belgium and the apparent ease with which the much-vaunted Belgian fortifications were destroyed partly hid the many problems faced by the Germans in the repair of bridges and railway tunnels demolished by the retreating Belgians. The disruption of the communications network would later hamper the movement of reinforcements to the German First and Second Armies during the crucial stages of the Battle of the Marne.

ABOVE: *Colonel General Helmut von Moltke, Germany's Chief of the General Staff and the man called upon to carry out the Schlieffen Plan.*

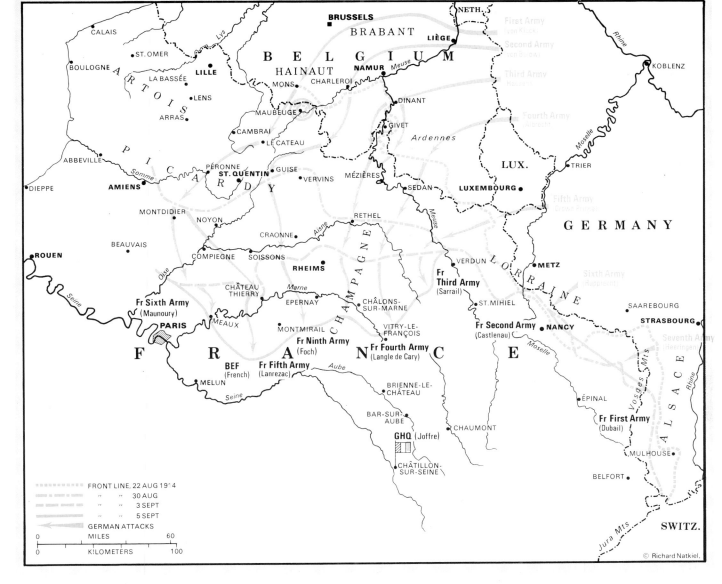

LEFT: *Germany's secret artillery weapon was the massive 42cm 'Big Bertha' howitzer manufactured by the world-famous armament company of Krupp. Along with the 30.5cm howitzers from Skoda, they smashed the Belgian forts that were the key elements within the great defensive complexes of Liège and Namur.*

RIGHT: *Belgium placed great faith in her extensive fortifications but the country's forces had been neglected. The 117,000-strong Belgian Army was poorly trained and led, and lacked the arms and equipment that were standard issue in the other armies of 1914. Here, the archaic appearance of the Belgian Army is emphasized by the dog-drawn machine-gun teams retreating toward Antwerp.*

BELOW: *As part of the occupation of Brussels, German horse-drawn transport passes through the city on 26 August 1914.*

BELOW RIGHT: *A hastily improvised barricade is manned by Belgian troops.*

A particular feature of the German advance through Belgium was their ruthless attitude toward any resistance from the Belgian people. The German Army pursued an official policy of *Schrecklichkeit* ('Frightfulness') to cow the local population into submission, thereby avoiding the need to leave large numbers of troops to guard rear communications. Well-documented instances of wholesale destruction and the killing of civilians took place throughout Belgium, perhaps the most notorious being the sacking of the medieval city of Louvain.

Oblivious to reports of the German advance into Belgium, General Joseph Joffre, the French Commander in Chief, undertook to fulfill the directives of Plan XVII. The sideshow in Alsace achieved little. After a series of attacks and counterattacks, the right flank of General Auguste Dubail's First Army was left clinging to a small strip of German territory near Mulhouse. The main offensive was spearheaded by the Second Army (General Noel de Castelnau) marching into Lorraine, supported by the remainder of Dubail's troops. Initially the Germans fell back, drawing in the over-confident French. On 20 August Crown Prince Rupprecht's Sixth Army launched a devastating counterattack – the Battles of Morhange and Sarrebourg – which saw the French thrown back to their own frontier within five days.

Farther north, the French Army fared little better. In an attempt to rupture the German center, Joffre ordered an advance into the Ardennes by the Third and Fourth Armies (Generals Ruffey and Langle de Cary). French reconnaissance was poor and in a confusing series of engagements the French were badly mauled.

General Charles Lanrezac (Fifth Army) was one of the few French commanders to perceive the intent of the German maneuver through Belgium and reluctantly obtained Joffre's permission to advance north to counter the threat. Alongside him was Britain's contribution to the land battle, the 110,000 men of the British Expeditionary Force (BEF) under Field Marshal Sir John French. On 22 August Kluck's First Army discovered the presence of the BEF, which had taken up position along the Mons-Condé Canal. On the following morning the Germans were stopped in their tracks by the rapid rifle fire of the British force, although outflanking movements forced the BEF to retire the following day. The French Fifth Army was already in full retreat and the BEF, with open flanks on both sides, was forced to fight a number of holding actions, including the costly Battle of Le Cateau, in order to ensure an orderly withdrawal southward to the Marne.

ABOVE: *Belgian villagers watch advance elements of the 2nd Scots Guards as they push deeper into Belgium, heading for an inevitable collision with the German forces along the Mons-Condé Canal.*

FAR LEFT: *General Joseph Joffre – he led his men to disaster by his adherence to Plan XVII in August 1914, but saved France in the following month by defeating the Germans.*

LEFT: *Field Marshal Sir John French, commander of the BEF from 1914 to 1915.*

RIGHT: *French returns a salute on his arrival at Boulogne on 14 August 1914.*

FAR RIGHT: *German cavalry escort French troops into captivity.*

ABOVE: *General Joseph Galliéni, the Military Governor of Paris and one of the architects of the French victory on the Marne.*

LEFT: *Men of the 1st Cameronians cross a pontoon bridge over the River Marne at La Ferte, 10 September 1914.*

BELOW LEFT: *Inter-Allied co-operation – troops of the 16th Lancers pass a unit of French cavalry during the great retreat.*

BELOW: *Sabres drawn, French cavalrymen escort German prisoners to the rear – here, fellow cavalrymen reduced to marching on foot.*

By 25 August the Allied position was critical: the French offensives had all failed dismally and the steadily advancing German columns were beginning to produce panic within government circles in Paris. Everywhere the French armies were in retreat. But at this moment of crisis Joffre's imperturbable resolution saved the situation. Now that Plan XVII was in ruins he set about organizing and encouraging his troops to counter the German advance. As a first step he began switching forces from eastern France by rail in order to form General Michael Joseph Maunoury's Sixth Army on the extreme Allied left. He then ordered the wavering Lanrezac, suffering from a crisis of confidence as his Fifth Army was increasingly exposed and outnumbered, to launch an attack between Guise and St Quentin. Despite reservations Lanrezac conducted the battle (29 August) with considerable skill. The engagement opened with a French attack on the German First Army, but when Bülow's Second Army pinned down the French right wing, Lanrezac coolly transferred his forces across the battlefront and inflicted a severe check on the Second Army. Bülow immediately requested assistance from Kluck's First Army, so that instead of swinging around Paris to the west as planned, the German First Army altered its direction south and due east of the French capital.

This maneuver meant the original Schlieffen Plan of 1905 was compromised, a blunder compounded by Moltke's decision to allow Rupprecht's Sixth Army to mount its own offensive in the hope of it being a left arm that would encircle rather than merely contain the French Army. Such opportunistic thinking was typical of Moltke's generalship. Rather than send reinforcements to his northern armies (which were desperately in need of

fresh troops), he tamely allowed Rupprecht, an aggressive though subordinate army commander, to dictate the strategic pace of the campaign.

The farther south the German First Army advanced, the more exposed its right wing became to a flank attack. By early September, Maunoury's Sixth Army was in place to the north of Paris. The military governor of the capital, General Joseph Simon Galliéni, called for an offensive by Maunoury's and his own forces on Kluck's flank. By 5 September the Allies had retired south of the Marne and at this point Joffre authorized Galliéni's proposal, also ordering an all-out counterattack along the entire French line.

The Battle of the Marne opened with Maunoury's assault on the German First Army along the River Ourq. Kluck's troops had little difficulty holding the French, but the movement of forces to his right flank opened up a gap between his and Bülow's Second Army. The strength of the French counterattack came as a shock to Moltke and, when the BEF and the French Fifth Army (now under the energetic leadership of General Louis Franchet d'Esperey) advanced into the gap, German resolution began to waver. On 8 September they began to retire.

So died the Schlieffen Plan, dashing German hopes of a 'battle without a morrow.' The first to pay the price of failure was Moltke, replaced as Chief of Staff on 14 September by the more able General Erich von Falkenhayn. The Battle of the Marne represented the triumph of superior French generalship. Joffre, despite the total collapse of Plan XVII, possessed the strength of mind and spirit to swiftly improvise a new plan for offensive action – once German intentions were known – which snatched victory from defeat. Joffre's refusal to panic and his close control of subordinate generals contrasted favorably with

Moltke's behavior during the battle which was characterized by an inability to co-ordinate the actions of his army commanders.

The Allied follow-up lacked vigor, however, thereby allowing the Germans to retreat in good order to defensive positions overlooking the River Aisne. The arrival of reserve formations bolstered the German line which held firm in spite of desperate attacks by the French and British on 13-14 September. The Germans were quick to build entrenchments and by the end of the month a stalemate had developed. As deadlock extended along the Franco-German line both sides commenced a series of outflanking maneuvers, progressing northward to the Belgian coast. Later dubbed the 'Race to the Sea,' the rapid deployment of reserves by both the Germans and the French prevented the possibility of a breakthrough by either side.

While the battle leapfrogged northward through France, Antwerp fell to the Germans on 9 October, although the Belgian Army extricated itself to take up a defensive position along the River Yser which then formed the northernmost section of the Allied line. As the area around the Yser had been flooded by the Belgians on 24 October, the advancing Germans looked to the open countryside further south, around the old Belgian town of Ypres, to effect a strategic thrust toward the vital Channel ports. Once again the BEF was to find itself in a key sector. Strengthened by reinforcements from England (to make a force of four army corps plus advance units of an Indian corps), British troops began arriving in Flanders on 12 October to take up position around the Belgian towns of Béthune, Armentières and Ypres. This sector of the front would see some bloody battles.

ABOVE LEFT: *Weary and cold, Belgian troops prepare for yet another day of hard marching.*

ABOVE: *Victims of the fighting – men and horses of the French Army begin to bloat in the summer sun.*

LEFT: *French infantrymen prepare to give fire in – for the standard of September 1914 – a well-dug trench.*

BELOW: *The first colonial troops arrive in France to aid the BEF. A column of Indian infantry marches up to the line at Ypres.*

The British Army at First Ypres

Throughout the history of warfare certain types of engagement have become known as 'Soldiers' Battles.' Characterized by a series of fierce encounters between forward troops, these battles are won more by the resolution and fighting skills of the common soldier than by the staff work and 'generalship' of the commander. Much of the fighting at the First Battle of Ypres in 1914 fell into the 'Soldiers' Battle' category and, even though the handling of reserves by the British commanders was superbly executed, the result was decided by the steadfastness of the British defense, supplemented by aggressive counterattacks.

The carnage on the Aisne and at Ypres had taken its toll: none of the 84 battalions of the BEF (British Expeditionary Force) was more than half its establishment strength by the middle of November 1914. Only two officers, two corporals and 27 men survived from the original 1000-strong 1st Battalion, Queen's Royal (West Surrey) Regiment, and these were mainly from the transport and cooking details. A total of 75 of the 84 battalions had been reduced to 300 officers and men or less in a period of four months. Britain's old professional army had been destroyed, although it had proved itself a magnificent fighting force in the process. The fighting had been ferocious. The views of one German reserve lieutenant were recorded thus:

> In the first few engagements our battalion was reduced to about half . . . We were at once struck with the great energy with which their infantry defended itself when driven back, and by the determined efforts made by it at night to recover lost ground . . . The main strength of the British undoubtedly lies in the defense and in the use of ground. Their nerves undoubtedly react better than those of the Germans, and their sporting instincts render them easier than our men to train in shooting, and in the use of ground and patrolling. The hardiness of their infantry was very apparent at (the First Battle of) Ypres. The shelter trenches were so well constructed that they could not be discovered with the naked eye . . . My own observation shows me that the British are excellent at patrol work, which I cannot say of our men.

A German chaplain, too, testified that the British were 'cold-blooded and tough and defend themselves even when their trenches are taken, quite different to the French.' Even the Kaiser had to admit in 1915 that I Corps of the BEF which had fought at Ypres was 'the best in the world.'

British troops face German positions around Gheluvelt, 20 October 1914.

LEFT: *German artillerymen with a 15cm howitzer, one of the most effective field pieces at the disposal of the German Army in 1914.*

RIGHT: *French Spahis escort German prisoners through the town of Furnes, November 1914.*

BELOW RIGHT: *Reflecting the grim conditions of the trenches around Ypres, British infantry prepare for a possible German attack.*

BELOW, FAR RIGHT: *British artillerymen prepare an 18-pounder for firing on the Armentières sector, 7 December 1914.*

The Christmas Truce 1914

One of the more surprising episodes of 1914 was the spontaneous Christmas Day truce which broke out among German and British troops along a number of sections of the line. To the horror of the High Command on both sides, weapons were laid aside as the troops mingled in No Man's Land, exchanging gifts and cigarettes, and playing football matches. It appears that it was the Germans who initiated the unofficial festive truce as this account from an anonymous British medical officer shows:

The most extraordinary scenes took place between the trenches. In front of our bit our men and the Germans got out of their trenches and mixed together, talking, exchanging cigarettes etc. Some of our people actually went into their trenches and stayed there for some time, being entertained by the enemy! All joined together in a sing-song, each side taking it in turn to sing a song, and finally they ended up with 'God Save The King' in which the Saxons sang most heartily! This is absolutely true. One of our men was given a bottle of wine in which to drink the King's health. The ——— Regiment actually had a football match with the Saxons, who beat them 3-2!

German and British soldiers fraternize at Ploegsteert, 25 December 1914.

Falkenhayn, settling upon Ypres as his area of operations, decided to launch one last great assault before the Allied line solidified. It was also at Ypres that the Franco-British forces attempted their last offensive of the campaign. Faced by superior German numbers and a far greater weight of German artillery, the Allied offensive came to a swift halt. From then on the Allies found themselves fighting a desperate defensive battle. Allied steadfastness and the timely arrival of French reinforcements were sufficient to weather the German storm. On 11 November the Germans made their last breakthrough attempt. Over 12 crack divisions – including the Prussian Guard – were held by the remnants of the Allied line. From then on the fighting died down as winter set in.

Losses were heavy on both sides. The Germans had thrown in the best of their reserve divisions, many of them formed from student volunteers whose enthusiasm and inexperience made them easy targets for the accurate rifle fire of the BEF. The Germans called the battle the 'Slaughter of the Innocents.' On the British side casualties were such that the regular Army was severely weakened. Over 50,000 British troops were killed. The heavily engaged 7th Division which went into the battle with an infantry strength of 12,300 was reduced to a complement of 2400 men. The First Battle of Ypres came to be known as the graveyard of the old British Army.

The German failure at the First Battle of Ypres was the final episode in the 1914 campaign in the West and represented a larger strategic defeat. Having failed to knock out the French in one decisive campaign the German High Command was now faced with the prospect of fighting a two-front war. Ypres also marked the end of a war of movement. After the battle the combatants began to dig in earnest, constructing an elaborate trench network along a line stretching 450 miles from Switzerland to the shores of the North Sea.

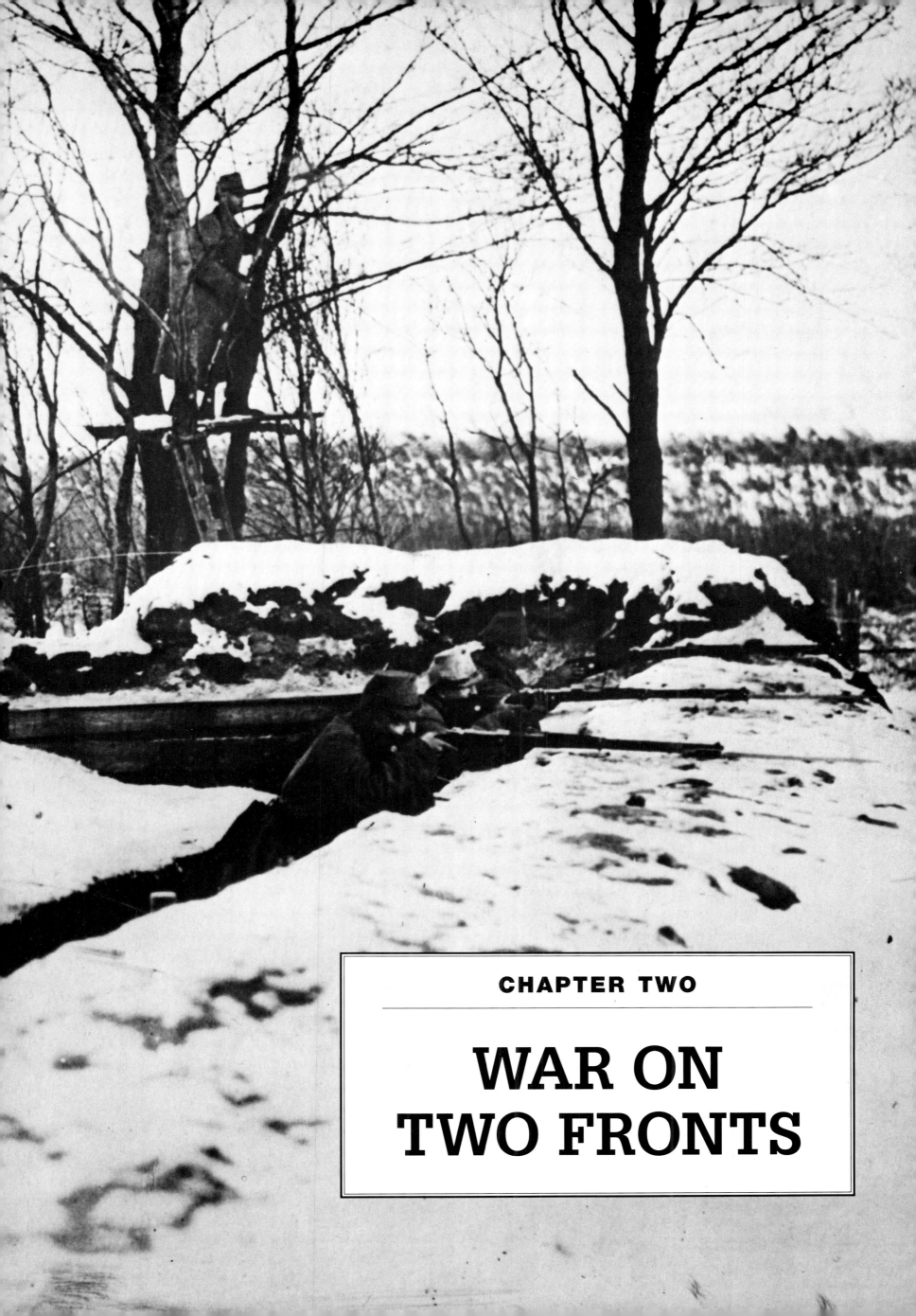

CHAPTER TWO

WAR ON
TWO FRONTS

The war on the Eastern Front was conducted over vast areas of eastern and central Europe, ranging across millions of square miles from the Baltic Sea in the north to the Black Sea in the south. As a consequence, the nature of the conflict took on a more fluid character than in the more geographically confined Western theater. Trench-bound deadlocks were few and temporary in nature, thereby allowing for the possibility of strategic maneuver. And yet, paradoxically, the great distances that the armies were forced to traverse – from the railhead, either on foot or horse – combined with the general resolution of the combatant nations not to give way (until 1917 at least), make it difficult to overcome the enemy outright. A defeated army could always retire and regroup or allow reinforcements to fill the gap. Thus, as in the West, the war became one of attrition.

The war in the East began with Austria-Hungary's punitive expedition against Serbia in August 1914. This was repulsed with contemptuous ease by the Serbs under the leadership of Field Marshal Radomir Putnik. The Serbian Army, while poorly equipped and comparatively small, consisted of determined and hardy troops fighting in defense of their homeland against a hated enemy. A second Austrian offensive in November ground to a halt only a few miles inside Serbia, and on 3 December the Serbs launched their own offensive which sent the Austrians fleeing back over the border. On the 15th a Serbian communiqué boasted: 'On the whole territory of the Serbian Government there remains not one free enemy soldier.' The deep humiliation suffered by Austria was compounded by the disasters which had taken place on the Eastern Front in the war against Russia.

Austria's strategic directive in the East called for an offensive northward from Galicia to cut off the Russian forces in the Polish salient. This was an ambitious plan, beyond the capabilities of the large, multi-national Army of the Austro-Hungarian Empire. Austrian planning relied on close co-operation with Germany, but this was not forthcoming as the German strategic plan for 1914 was based around a major offensive against France, while in the East German forces were to remain on the defensive until troops could be released from the Western Front. Only one army (the Eighth, under General Max von Prittwitz und Gaffron) was deployed to guard East Prussia.

Russia had a great advantage in her vast resources of manpower. With a peacetime strength of over a million men the Russian Army would be able to deploy four million men once full mobilization had taken place. Beside manpower, Russia also possessed enormous material resources and during the period leading up to the outbreak of war heavy industry had made rapid progress, to the extent that the nation was on the verge of becoming a real industrial giant. Set against this great potential there were, however, many disadvantages. The sheer size of the Russian Empire and its relatively poor rail communications slowed mobilization, making the rapid transport of reserves from front to front a cumbersome process. Far worse than these geographical problems, however, was the incompetence, corruption and departmental rivalry endemic to the Russian bureaucracy.

In some respects the Russian Army was of a high caliber: its arms and equipment were of a comparable standard to those of other European powers and there was a sprinkling of able officers at all levels of command. Yet like the civil administration it was bedeviled by inter-service rivalries, logistic ineptitude and administrative corruption. There was no effective high command structure (similar to the German General Staff) for an Army numbering millions, and invariably the dead hand of reaction stifled any initiative. Political appointments to senior posts were the order of the day and military ability often counted for little. At the same time, however, the Russian Army produced in General Alexei Brusilov one of the most able commanders of the war on any side. Certainly, the Russian Army of 1914 was one of contrasts.

The Russian plan envisaged that the main weight of the 1914 offensive would be directed against Austria. However, because of the pleas of her French ally, desperately wanting to divert German troops away from the Western Front, the plans were modified to include an immediate invasion of East Prussia. The offensive into East Prussia fell to Army Group Jilinsky, consisting of the First Army (General Pavel Rennenkampf), which would attack from the east, and the Second Army (General Alexander Samsonov), poised on the German southern flank. On 20 August, Rennenkampf scored a minor tactical victory at Gumbinnen which threw Prittwitz into a temporary battlefield panic.

PREVIOUS PAGES: German troops keep watch from carefully prepared positions near the Masurian Lakes in East Prussia. Anticipating a possible Russian advance into this area, the Germans constructed a series of interconnected strongpoints to blunt any invasion.

ABOVE: General Pavel Rennenkampf, the incompetent commander of the Russian First Army.

RIGHT: Russian troops of the First Army march through a German town in East Prussia during the early days of their offensive.

BELOW: Russian peasants are mobilized to become part of a reserve formation in the town of Bogorodsk.

BELOW RIGHT: German cavalry on a reconnaissance mission near Willkijmien, East Prussia, September 1914.

ABOVE: The lull before the storm – German troops remove lice from their uniforms.

Prittwitz's suggestion that East Prussia be abandoned led Moltke to promptly sack him, sending as his replacement the venerable 68-year-old Colonel General Paul von Hindenburg with Major General Erich Ludendorff as his Chief of Staff. Although they were outnumbered, the Germans had several advantages. The two Russian armies were operating in virtual isolation from each other and their radio transmissions were often sent uncoded, allowing the Germans to 'overhear' their plans and dispositions. Exploiting their strategic railways, the Germans adopted the proposal of a junior staff officer, Colonel Max

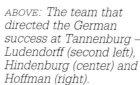

ABOVE: The team that directed the German success at Tannenburg – Ludendorff (second left), Hindenburg (center) and Hoffman (right).

ABOVE LEFT: A few of the thousands of Russians captured by the Germans during the campaign in East Prussia.

LEFT: A dramatic action shot of German infantry under artillery fire.

BELOW: General Nikolai Ivanoff, commander of the Southern Army Group that won a major victory over the Austrians in Galicia.

von Hoffman, and concentrated against Samsonov's forces in the south.

Despite his relatively junior rank, Hoffman was a talented strategist and he had gained a thorough knowledge of the workings of the Russian Army while acting as an observer with the Japanese Army during the war against Russia in 1904. Consequently he was aware of the long-standing enmity between Samsonov and Rennenkampf and (correctly) reasoned that Rennenkampf would not be quick to come to his colleague's aid.

The German Eighth Army caught Samsonov's forces scattered around the village of Tannenberg on 26 August, and in a four-day battle of encirclement completely destroyed the Russian Second Army. The completeness of the German victory – they captured some 120,000 Russians – owed much to the skills of the German corps commanders, especially the aggressive and independent-minded General Hermann von François (I Corps) who, repeatedly disregarding Army HQ orders, was responsible for the encirclement of the Russians. Samsonov committed suicide, the remains of his army reeling back into Russian Poland. Using their railways once more, the Germans turned eastward and pushed Rennenkampf out of East Prussia in the first week of September in a complex series of engagements later called the Battle of the Masurian Lakes.

Although heavily defeated in the north, the Russians fared better in the south against Austria. General Conrad von Hötzendorf, the Austrian Chief of Staff, launched his offensive northward into Poland during the last week of August, only to be caught in the flank by the Russian Southern Army Group commanded by General Nikolai Ivanoff. The Austrians retreated in confusion, losing

ABOVE: Employing log
barriers and loopholed steel
plates, German troops look
across to Russian positions
in the Masurian Lakes area
of East Prussia. This is one
of the many strongpoints
built by the Germans before
the war as part of a series of
defenses to blunt any
Russian offensive.

ABOVE RIGHT: A Russian
battery is prepared for
action against the Austrian
fortress of Przemysl during
the Galician campaign of
late 1914.

LEFT: Austrian troops man
an improvised position in
the Carpathians in the
winter of 1914 after having
been driven out of Galicia
by the Russian armies of
Ivanoff's army group. This
was a major disaster for the
Austrians.

almost all of Galicia (including the empire's fourth city, Lemberg) and some 350,000 men in the process. It was a crippling defeat. The poor performance of Austria's troops came as a shock to the Germans ('We are shackled to a corpse,' noted one acid-tongued observer) and with it came the unwelcome realization that they would have to bolster up their weakened ally. To this end, German divisions were transferred from the Western Front in October to form the Ninth Army which was then added to Hindenburg's growing command.

The disaster of the expedition against Serbia and the first campaign against Russia revealed the many imperfections within the Austro-Hungarian Army. While following the German mold in outward form, it was very different in reality. The acquisition by the twin kingdoms of Austria and Hungary of a polyglot and multi-racial empire in the Balkans was the root cause of its inability to wage a modern war in the twentieth century. The imposition of universal military suffrage throughout the empire engendered the resentment of the Slav populations and ensured the deterioration of the military standards set in the German-Magyar partnership. The emergence of the self-conscious nationalist ideologies during the nineteenth century ensured that many soldiers within the Austro-Hungarian Army shared a racial kinship with the empire's enemies. By 1914 the Austro-Hungarian Empire

Atrocities of War

The racial tensions that existed between the Germanic element of the Austro-Hungarian Empire and Slavic Serbia exploded once war was declared. The Austrian invasion of Serbia was deliberately planned as a punitive expedition: hostages were taken from the civilian population and any sign of civil disobedience met with vicious reprisal. The Austrians exercised minimal control over their troops' behavior toward the Serbian population and atrocities were widespread. Although coming from a partisan source, this Serbian officer's report was later verified by observers from other nations:

A group of children, girls, women and men, 15 in all, were lying dead, tied together by their hands. Most of them had been bayoneted. One young girl had been bayoneted below the jaw, on the left, and the point of the weapon had come out through the right cheekbone. Many of the corpses had no teeth left. On the back of an old woman who was lying on her face, there was some coagulated blood, and in this were found some teeth. This old woman was lying beside the girl whose wound has been described above. It would appear that the old woman was killed first, and the young girl immediately afterward, so that the teeth of the latter were scattered on the back of the old woman. The chemises of the little girls and young women were bloodstained, which seemed to indicate that they had been violated before being killed. Near this group, apart, lay the dead bodies of three men who had been bayoneted in the head, throat and cheek.

COLONEL DOKITCH,
20th Serbian Infantry Regiment.

The Cancer of Corruption

Of the many problems facing Russia during World War I, none was worse than the corruption that seemed to exist at all levels of society and across the entire country. The most notable offender was General Sukhomlinov, Minister of War. His avarice was fueled by the demands of an extravagant young wife. The prerogatives of patronage open to a minister of war were enormous during wartime, but Sukhomlinov supplemented this bread-and-butter corruption with the straight swap of confidential information for extra lavish 'gifts.' Among these friends and beneficiaries of Sukhomlinov was Austria's top secret agent, a Russian railway policeman in league with Germany. Despite all this, Sukhomlinov retained his position until March 1917, when the Provisional Government caught up with him and sentenced him to life imprisonment with hard labor. However, the wily operator remained one step ahead of the authorities and, following the Bolshevik Revolution, Sukhomlinov was able to obtain his release. He subsequently fled to Berlin.

General B A Sukhomlinov.

had become a dangerous anachronism, one poised to burst apart at the seams.

Beside this problem of racial diversity, Austria-Hungary also lacked the industrial base necessary to fight a prolonged war in which the daily expenditure of shells and bullets numbered millions. The empire's stocks of munitions, capable of sustaining the 'short' wars of the nineteenth century, were soon used up in the battles of 1914 and from then on the Army suffered from shortages – always chronic and sometimes acute. Leadership was another weakness in the Austro-Hungarian system. Conrad von Hötzendorf was highly regarded for his strategic ability but in reality he was a 'maps and paper' general and his grandiose plans came to little.

Considering the poor overall stability and quality of the Austro-Hungarian Empire and its Army, perhaps the most surprising fact was that it held out until the summer of 1918. On a purely military level, it was obvious by 1915 that Austria's Army was incapable of sustained offensive action, but with German support it could carry on defensive operations. This became the essential strategy of the Central Powers for the rest of the war. Any offensive operation would be a direct German responsibility.

During the Fall of 1914 great pendulum swings of battle succeeded each other on the Eastern Front. The Russians forced the Austrians back to the Carpathian Mountains and threatened German Silesia. But by mid-November the Russian advance had lost momentum, largely through shortages of supplies and munitions, and General August von Mackensen's counterattack around Lodz (18-25 November) pushed the Russians back to the Vistula.

As Commander in Chief of all German forces in the

RIGHT: General August von Mackensen.

FAR RIGHT: Russian field artillery in position in the Carpathian Mountains.

BELOW: Russian infantry doggedly struggle through wire entanglements during an attack in western Poland.

BELOW RIGHT: German infantry march into Russian territory during the great offensive of 1916.

LEFT: Austrian troops move up a mountain pass in the Carpathians. The winter campaign of 1914 was renowned for the bitterness of the fighting and atrocious weather conditions.

BELOW LEFT: An Austro-Hungarian field-gun battery is prepared for action in defense of a mountain village.

RIGHT: Russian soldiers stand guard in a frontline trench by the Panevezhskaya railway on the Dvina Front. Although well constructed, the trench has not got the traverses and fire-bays of a Western Front trench.

BELOW: An Austrian soldier poses by the corpse of a Russian caught and hanged on the charge of spying. The Austrians – like their German ally – were quick to impose draconian punishments on the enemy population under their control.

BELOW RIGHT: Czar Nicholas II (second left) arrives by automobile to meet frontline troops. The Russian Commander in Chief, Grand Duke Nicholas, stands in the car (far right).

East, Hindenburg soon found himself at variance with Falkenhayn, the German Chief of Staff, whose attentions were directed toward other theaters of war. Hindenburg argued for massive reinforcements to deliver a knock-out blow against the Russians by encircling their forces in the Polish salient in the Fall of 1914. However, the demands for troops in the West forced the Germans to adopt a more circumspect approach. In 1915 the stalemate in the West and the plight of the Austrians forced Falkenhayn to adopt a new strategy, a major effort against Russia. Fighting of a most desperate nature took place all winter in sub-zero temperatures in the Carpathians, but the first important move came in February 1915 with a limited German attack from East Prussia known as the Winter Battle in Masuria.

The Russian spring offensive of 1915 under the direct command of Grand Duke Nicholas was directed at the Austrians along the Carpathians. The Central Powers' fear that the Russians might break through into the Hungarian plain meant German action was essential. Falkenhayn decided upon an offensive in the area just north of the Carpathian Mountains, between the Vistula and San Rivers. Not only would this relieve the hard-pressed Austrians, it would also threaten the Russian forces in the Polish salient. The spearhead of the attack would be the eight German divisions transported from France in the newly constituted Eleventh Army (Colonel General August von Mackensen). Mackensen's Chief of Staff, Colonel Hans von Seeckt, masterminded the plan of attack in which a concentrated breakthrough would be followed up by a rapid exploitation to deny the Russians any chance to recover and stabilize the line.

The German troops were transferred from the West in

April and on the 27th they were in position between the towns of Gorlice and Tarnow, from where the main assault would be launched. The Russian line in this area was relatively well-defended. Three lines of trenches formed a belt some 10 miles deep and, accordingly, Mackensen brought up 700 guns to paralyze the Russian lines before the German infantry went over the top.

After a short but violent bombardment on the morning of 2 May, German troops advanced across No Man's Land, occupying the wrecked Russian trenches with almost no resistance. Once a gap had been made in the Russian line, German reinforcements flooded through; Seeckt ordered that 'all staffs must strive to keep the advance continuously moving.' The infantry pushed on with utmost speed, forcing the disordered Russians to fall back in order not to be cut off. This strategy succeeded beyond expectation and anticipated the infiltration tactics of the 1918 offensive in the West. Within two weeks, advance forces had penetrated to a depth of nearly 100 miles – a notable feat by any standards, but one which must have astounded the trenchbound soldiers in France.

By the end of May, the Russians had been forced back behind the San and Dniester Rivers, but there they found only temporary respite as more German reinforcements crossed both rivers to clear the Russians from Galicia during June. The momentum of the offensive was such that Falkenhayn felt obliged to push on further, wheeling northward to cut off the Russians in Warsaw. Falkenhayn also ordered an advance southward from East Prussia to surround the Russian forces in the increasingly beleaguered Polish salient, while Mackensen continued to advance northward from Galicia. German success was less than total, however. The northern arm of the great pincer movement was held up for two weeks by Russian forces along the River Narew, thereby allowing Grand Duke Nicholas to withdraw most of his troops from the trap. Warsaw fell on 4 August, a great propaganda triumph for the Germans who then pushed on to capture the railway junction of Brest-Litovsk, some 125 miles east of the Polish capital.

ABOVE LEFT: After the great success of the Gorlice-Tarnow breakthrough, German cavalry was kept fully employed in escorting and guarding the tens of thousands of Russian prisoners cut off by the German advance.

LEFT: Yet more prisoners. Russian captives are herded back to the rear while German infantry march forward, pushing deeper into Russian territory.

The German command team: Hindenburg, the Kaiser and Ludendorff.

The German General Staff

All armies require the services of a general staff in order to carry out the orders of their commanders and ensure the smooth running of a vast human organization often working in the most difficult of circumstances. In peacetime the main function of the general staff is to plan the appropriate strategy for a war in the future. As the size of armies grew, so the size and importance of the general staff increased to the extent that it controlled all Army life.

The German General Staff was the direct successor (after the creation of the German Empire in 1871) to the Prussian General Staff which had played such an important role in Prussia's rise to dominance in central Europe during the mid-nineteenth century. Under the command of Field Marshal Helmut von Moltke (the elder), the General Staff rose to a position of unique importance within the German armed forces. As Chief of Staff, Moltke's careful planning was largely responsible for the great victories over Austria in 1866 and France in 1870, and the General Staff began to be seen as the catalyst for victory. In the years between the Franco-Prussian War of 1870-71 and the final outbreak of war in 1914, the General Staff grew in size and importance. It attracted the most intelligent young officers within the German Army and only the best were able to gain admission to this prestigious organization. For the ambitious officer, the General Staff was considered one of the swiftest means to promotion and the gaining of key positions within the army hierarchy. Thus in Germany a position on the staff was to be envied, whereas in most other European armies the reputation of their general staffs was much lower and most kudos was associated with field command appointments. However the success of the German Army in the nineteenth century began to force a change of attitude and, in the years leading up to the 1914, the general staffs of all armies were increasingly influenced by the German system.

One of the more significant aspects of the German General Staff – and, surprisingly, of the German Army in general – was the influence of relatively junior officers on major decision-making in war-time. Officers of the rank of major or colonel were sent on roving commissions from the General Staff to the various army headquarters, gaining information from the troops on the spot and relaying directives from the Chief of Staff. In addition they were able to interpret General Staff orders in the light of events and possibly overrule an army commander, even though he might be a senior general. The most famous example of these powers occurred during the Battle of the Marne in 1914 when a staff officer, Lieutenant Colonel Hentsch, ordered General von Kluck's First Army to break off hostilities and retire – arguably the most important decision made during the entire battle.

Although the General Staff was a large semi-autonomous institution during World War I, it remained a reflection of its Chief of Staff. Under Moltke (the younger), it lacked authority, thereby allowing subordinate commanders a greater role in the direction of the fighting than was desirable. His successor, Falkenhayn, was a stronger person and imposed his stamp of leadership on all his subordinates. However, his view of the Western Front as *the* theater of decision alienated the German commanders on the Eastern Front, notably the team of Hindenburg and Ludendorff who, in turn, succeeded Falkenhayn in 1916. Although more evenhanded in their assessment of the respective merits of Western and Eastern strategic plans, they eventually followed Falkenhayn in accepting the primacy of war in the West.

The German General Staff had always been a most powerful institution within Germany but during the course of the war it progressively assumed new powers and responsibilities to the extent that Hindenburg and Ludendorff became the *de facto* rulers of Germany and those lands under its control. The Kaiser, the German Parliament and other forms of civil administration were pushed aside by the General Staff which, in the last year of the war, was dictating Germany's military, civil and foreign policy. Such responsibilities were beyond the capabilities of the General Staff and its inability to make the appropriate decisions only hastened German's inevitable collapse.

By the beginning of September the offensive was drawing to a close. Falkenhayn wished to stabilize the line and construct winter quarters before the weather broke and the battlegrounds turned to mud. Localized offensives were conducted by Hindenburg in the north – his forces secured Vilna on 18 September – while in the south Hötzendorf pushed his Austrian troops into the Ukraine only to have them severely mauled by a Russian counter-attack. Once the Austrians had again been rescued by the transfer of German divisions in October, the fighting died down.

The Austro-German forces had made massive gains: they had advanced nearly 300 miles and inflicted an estimated 2,000,000 casualties on the Russians. To almost any other nation such a defeat would have been a mortal blow. Russia, however, not only survived but accelerated the expansion of its war industries. Military supplies were stockpiled and by the following year the army was even considering offensive operations.

The controversy within the German High Command between the 'Westerner' Falkenhayn and the 'Easterners' Hindenburg and Ludendorff continued unabated throughout 1915. Although Falkenhayn had readily agreed to the Gorlice-Tarnow breakthrough, he nonetheless had refused to allow the Eastern High Command a blank check to carry on the offensive into the Fall of 1915. Despite the heavy casualties suffered by the Russians, their Army was still intact and, as Falkenhayn argued, able to draw the Germans further into the Russia heartlands and thereby to dangerously overextend them. In addition, Falkenhayn had to consider other demands on German resources, one of which was the co-ordination of a major offensive against Serbia.

In the south, Serbia remained a thorn in the side of the Central Powers throughout 1915, but when they signed a treaty with Bulgaria on 6 September 1915, plans were drawn up to destroy the Serbian irritant for good. Mackensen, newly promoted to Field Marshal, was sent to direct the combined Austro-German-Bulgarian forces in the field. In October Austro-German armies invaded Serbia from the north while two Bulgarian armies struck across the border in the east. Outnumbered and outflanked, the Serbs – soldiers and civilians together – were forced to retreat westward through the mountains of Albania.

The march was an epic of endurance. Besides being pursued by the advancing Bulgarians, the Serbs had to contend with bitterly cold weather as they slowly made their way across the mountains. Exhausted and weakened by cold and hunger, typhus broke out, further reducing the ranks. Yet the retreating Serbs maintained good order throughout and were even able to transport 25,000 Austrian prisoners to a new captivity beyond the Balkans. British and French forces landed at Salonika in Greece, but their advance was successfully barred by the Bulgarians. Anglo-French troopships were sent to pick up the survivors of the grueling trek, but this was the only help the western powers could offer their Balkan ally, and consequently 1915 saw the end of 'plucky little Serbia.' The remnants of the Serbian Army were transported to Salonika to form part of the Allied force there. The strength of the Central Powers in the Balkans, combined with Allied inactivity, ensured that the Serbs could do little to liberate their homeland until the final offensives of 1918.

As the year 1915 drew to a close, Falkenhayn could take some satisfaction from the success of his strategy. In the West and against Turkey, the Allied assaults had been contained, while in the East the Germans had inflicted a substantial defeat on the Russians and, in the process, gained control of a considerable portion of Russia's western territories. Once again the Austrians had been carried by their German ally, although at least in the overrunning of Serbia they had avenged the insult of Sarajevo.

The Russians had suffered grievous casualties since 1914 and the morale of their Army had been badly shaken. Some Russian officers now began to feel they were powerless to stop the Germans; their own offensives failed miserably while those of their enemy invariably met with success. This mood of despondency was not universal, but the great losses of 1915 marked the beginning of the slide toward collapse and revolution in 1917.

RIGHT: *The dead lie where they fell, a few of the casualties of the Austro-German-Bulgarian advance into Serbia. Against such a well-organized and concerted operation, the Serbians had no chance.*

BELOW: *Another capital city falls to German arms – a cavalry detachment rides through the streets of Warsaw in August 1915.*

BELOW RIGHT: *The horror of the Serbian retreat through Montenegro – the Serbian baggage train struggles through a mountain pass deep in the grip of winter.*

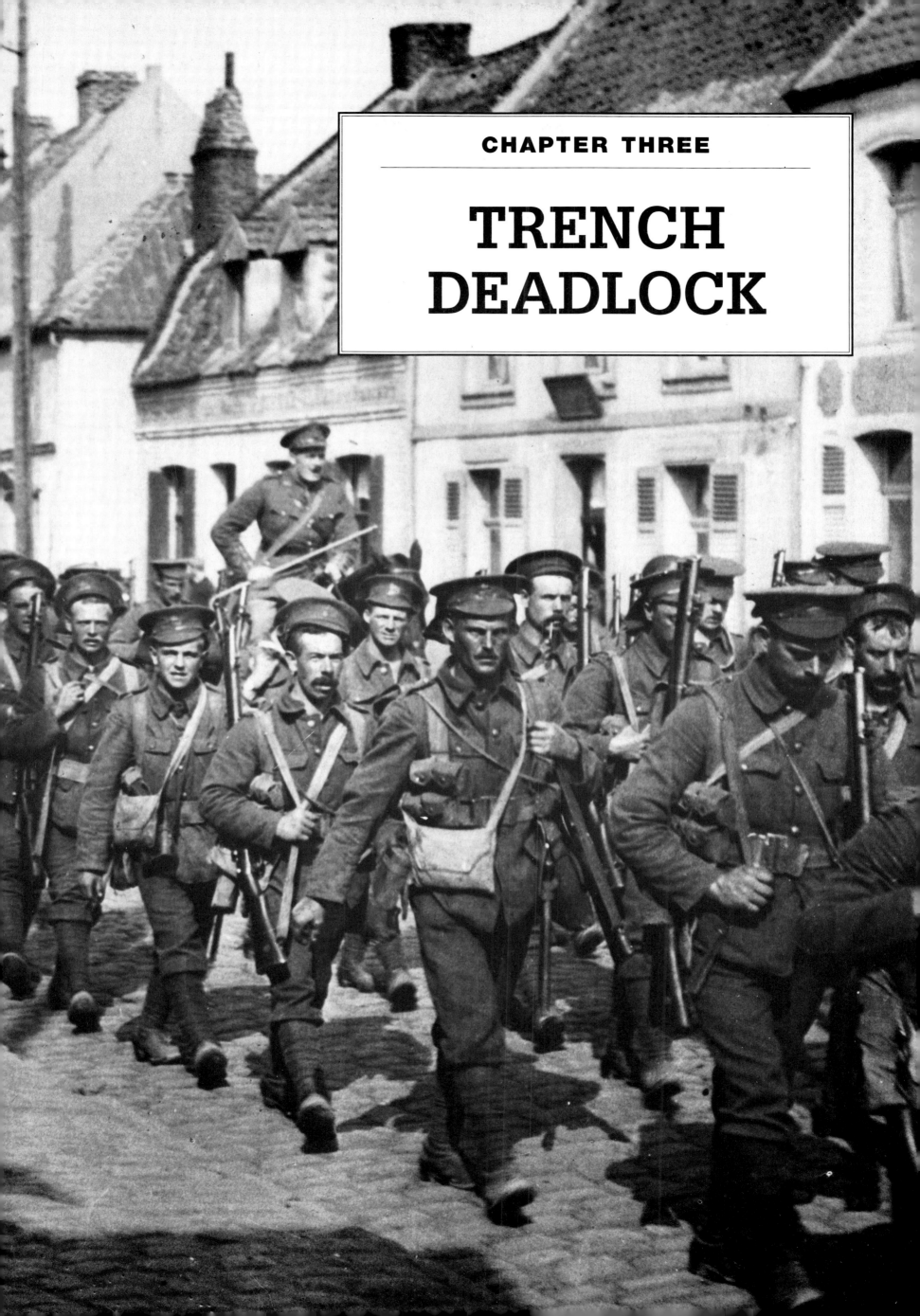

CHAPTER THREE

TRENCH DEADLOCK

As the conflict entered its second year, the old eager hopes that the war would be decided within six months had clearly been shattered. 'It'll all be over by Christmas,' had been a common 1914 catchphrase. Even though the Chiefs of Staff pored over their maps and plans hoping to deliver a knock-out blow, the governments of the opposing nations reluctantly began to prepare for all-out war in which victory would go to the side that could hang on the longest. In the West the strategic initiative lay with Germany: her armies were in possession of Belgium (save for a narrow strip around Ypres) and France's industrial centers in the northeast. Coal shortages, for example, were a perennial problem for the French throughout the war. In addition, the German presence was an intolerable affront to French nationalist sensibilities and consequently the only possible strategy for the Allies was offensive action at all levels. On the other side of the line, the German Chief of Staff, General von Falkenhayn, ultimately placed his faith upon a decision against France and Britain. His plan of campaign for 1915, however, consisted of an attritional defense in the West, so that the main weight of Germany's military resources could be deployed against the Russians.

Despite an expansion in size, the British Expeditionary Force (BEF) remained the junior partner of the Entente, understandably falling in line with French directives. In France the British commanders were confident that victory lay on the Western Front; the government was less sure, and with the passage of time, the generals' claims were regarded with increased skepticism. By the end of 1915 vast numbers of British troops would be ready for war. Lord Kitchener's hypnotic appeal for a volunteer 'million army' had been fulfilled by December 1914 and was subsequently to grow to 3,621,045 men. This led to the dilemma of where best to employ them. Many British politicians, shocked by the rising casualty lists from France and Flanders, looked toward operations in the Middle East as a means of employing the volunteers.

From 1915 onward, there were frequent and bitter arguments among British strategists: on the one side the 'Westerners' considered the main and decisive war front to be in the West; on the other side, the 'Easterners' urged

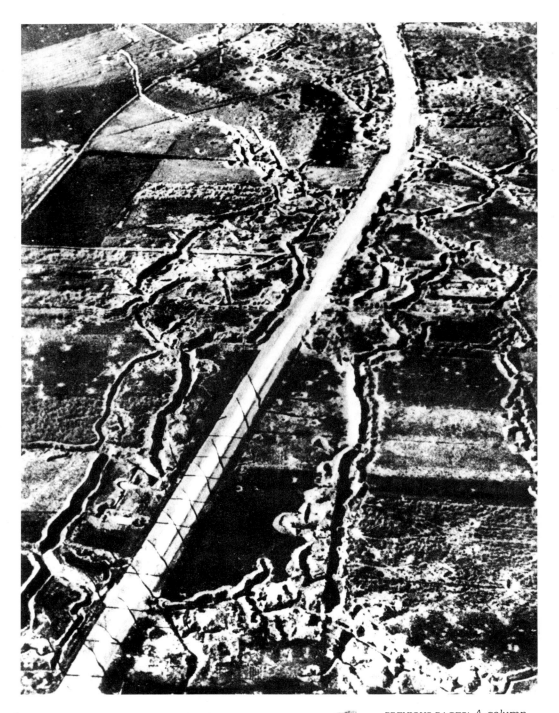

PREVIOUS PAGES: *A column of British infantry marches through the streets of a small French town after the Battle of Loos, September 1915. An unsuccessful battle for the British, Loos revealed many shortcomings in organization and leadership.*

ABOVE: *A German aerial photograph of May 1915 reveals the development of the trench system (to become ever more complex as the war progressed) of the German line at Zonnebeke in the Ypres sector.*

LEFT: *German troops of the 27th Regiment occupy a fire-trench in front of Allied positions at Arras during the winter of 1914-15. An unusual feature is the improvised revetment of the trench built with pieces of wood from packing cases.*

ABOVE: Men of the 11th Hussars stand in front of a brazier in trenches near Zillebeke, February 1915. As the war of movement ended so cavalry regiments moved into the trenches alongside the infantry.

attacks on Austria and Turkey. Regardless of the outcome of the debate, Kitchener's volunteers had to be trained and equipped, which was a slow process. For most of 1915 the remnants of the Old Army held the line, supported by the territorials, troops drawn from overseas garrisons and contingents from India and Canada. The essential problem facing French and British commanders was how to breach the German Army's fortifications. By the spring of 1915 they had constructed an extensive trench network which was becoming ever more complex as the months went by, thereby increasing the already formidable power of the defense.

The trench system on the Western Front varied considerably, according to the underlying terrain, but typically might consist of a frontline fire-trench, out of which ran a series of saps toward the enemy position providing 'jumping-off' points for an assault. In the case of

defensive action, the saps provided vantage points for enfilade fire. Behind the fire-trench ran two or more support lines (where the main body of frontline troops would be stationed), connected to each other by a series of communication trenches running at right angles to the main trenches. These were dug in a zig-zag pattern to prevent enfilade fire should the enemy penetrate the system. The trenches themselves were simply a means of protecting the infantrymen; the enemy was prevented from crossing the gap between the opposing lines – No Man's Land – by the artillery, rifles and machine guns of the defenders. Barbed wire, an entangling device that invariably brought the swiftest advance to a highly vulnerable standstill, was used in vast quantities.

As the war continued, trench systems on both sides became more complicated. In wet areas they had to be built up above ground using innumerable sandbags. In

mountainous districts, such as the Vosges, they were tunneled out of the rock. The Germans, normally on the defensive, showed particular ingenuity, making good use of the mining and digging equipment that had originally been intended for siege work. Later, they used reinforced concrete on a lavish scale for the construction of deep dugouts and fortified strongpoints, the latter known as 'pill-boxes' by virtue of their appearance.

Although facing the extensive German trench network, the Allies tried to seize back the strategic initiative they had lost at the beginning of the war. However, in 1915 they were woefully deficient in the materials necessary for the waging of trench warfare. Whereas the Germans were well supplied with howitzers, trench mortars and hand grenades, for example, the French and British were often forced to improvise. The Allied shortage of heavy artillery and, even worse, sufficient ammunition stocks was to be a major cause for concern throughout 1915.

In February and March 1915 the French launched further offensives against the Germans in Champagne, the final stages of the 'Winter Battle in Champagne' which had begun in December 1914. The result was heavy casualties for small gains. Unabashed by these losses the French Commander in Chief, General Joffre, continued his policy of 'nibbling the enemy to death,' so that in April 64,000 men were sacrificed in the unsuccessful assault on the St Mihiel salient.

The British, still small in numbers and lacking equipment, could do little to help their French ally and the

LEFT: *A column of German infantry marches by snow-covered trees toward the front line, March 1915.*

ABOVE: *General Sir Horace Smith-Dorrien, commander of the British Second Army.*

RIGHT: *British troops take over a smashed trench in the Bridoux-Rouges Bancs sector, February 1915.*

BELOW: *Corpses lie scattered in No Man's Land, following the British offensive at Neuve Chapelle, March 1915.*

resulting strain on the coalition became serious. Largely to counteract the French dismissal of the British Army's ability to wage offensive warfare, it was decided that the BEF should launch an attack against Neuve Chapelle, between Lens and Armentières. The BEF was now divided into two armies: First (Sir Douglas Haig) and Second (General Sir Horace Smith-Dorrien). Haig's army was entrusted with the assault.

Haig's preparations were carried out with methodical care and his plan of battle was highly innovative. Photographic reconnaissance from the air provided detailed maps of the enemy trenches; these were issued to all officers involved in the offensive. Artillery timetables were introduced, special gun platforms were built to provide stability on soft ground and a short whirlwind bombardment was planned before the assault, though a shortage of ammunition was the determining factor in this. Secrecy was carefully preserved in the hope of surprising the Germans on the day of battle, and the infantry were rehearsed in carrying out the tasks that lay ahead.

On the morning of 10 March the battle opened with a 35-minute bombardment of the German front line, after which the artillery's range was lengthened to form a 'curtain of fire' around the main battle zone in an attempt to inhibit the movement of German reinforcements. As the barrage moved forward the 14 battalions of the assault force advanced across No Man's Land and quickly overran the battered German frontline trenches. A breakthrough seemed possible, but after the initial success the advance

Punishment

Punishment, or the threat of punishment, has always been an important element within any army's range of coercive powers. By its very nature military discipline has to be stricter than civil discipline, with the failure to obey orders being the greatest crime. The approach to discipline varied from army to army in World War I, reflecting deep-seated national differences. Thus, for example, although the French and British armed forces shared a central core of attitudes toward discipline and punishment, there were many variations in the details.

Failure to obey orders was punished by court-martial or by the administration of summary justice by commanding officers in both the French and British Armies, although their methods differed. Discipline in the French Army was stern but not overbearing and did not seek to humiliate the offender; however British Army practice did. For cowardice in the face of the enemy, desertion and mutiny, the punishment was death in both armies. The British punished lesser crimes of a serious nature with Number One Field Punishment – the dirtiest and most unpleasant tasks followed by two hours per day chained to a wagon wheel for up to 21 days – a practice that was utterly abhorrent to the traditions of the French Army and the one most resented by the British rank and file. British officers were not usually vindictive, but men who were charged were generally convicted. One battalion which fought in the Battle of the Aisne in September 1914 was punished by its commanding officer for a lackluster performance with one execution (for cowardice) and Number One Field Punishment for all stragglers.

Although relations between French officers and men were more paternal, a draconian atmosphere set in under the strain of the failures of 1914-15. On 6 September 1914 the French Government passed a decree setting up *cours martiales* to try men accused of looting, desertion and self-mutilation on the spot. The disciplinary bodies consisted of seven officers who could convene the court immediately and punish offenders once they had been found guilty. This system was open to abuse and put conscripted men at the mercy of any officers with the rank to convene a *cour martiale*.

One example of the dangers of this system was revealed in what became known as 'the affair of the four corporals of Suippes.' In March 1915 the 21st Company of the 336th Regiment refused to join an attack at Perthes-les-Hurlus in Champagne. The divisional commander was furious and ordered the 21st Company commander to send four corporals and 16 privates on a suicidal mission. Under the stream of fire which met them, these men took cover in shell holes and returned to their own lines after dark. The divisional commander immediately convened a *cour martiale* and the 20 men were sentenced to death *pour l'exemple*. The general then had second thoughts and decided that only four corporals should be shot. The firing squad was less than enthusiastic about their duty and two of the corporals had to be finished off by the officer in charge, just before a reprieve arrived from the repentant divisional commander. This sort of summary (and morale-sapping) justice was, on the whole, absent from the disciplinary methods of the British Army.

LEFT: *A company of Zouaves moves up a road toward the front. Like Britain, France made considerable use of soldiers from her colonies, some of whom were counted among the elite of the French Army. It was an Algerian division that first experienced the horror of a gas attack.*

RIGHT: *A British first aid man attends a wounded soldier during a gas attack.*

Gas Attack

The use of gas during the opening part of an offensive proved to be — at least at first — a devastating weapon, as this British account reveals:

As we gazed in the direction of the bombardment where our line joined the French six miles away, we could see in the failing light the flash of shrapnel with, here and there, the light of a rocket. But more curious than anything else was a low cloud of yellow-grey smoke or vapor and, underlying everything, a dull confused murmuring. Suddenly down the road from the Yser Canal came a galloping team of horses, the riders goading on their mounts in a frenzied way; then another and another, till the road became a seething mass with a pall of dust over all.

Plainly something terrible was happening. What was it? Officers, and staff officers too, stood gazing at the scene, awestruck and dumbfounded; for on the northerly breeze there came a pungent, nauseating smell that tickled the throat and made our eyes smart. The horses and men were still pouring down the road, two or three on a horse, I saw, while over the fields streamed mobs of infantry, the dusky warriors of French Africa; away went their rifles, equipment, even their tunics that they might run the faster. One man came stumbling through our lines. An officer of ours held him up with a leveled revolver. 'What's the matter, you bloody lot of cowards?' says he. The Zouave was frothing at the mouth, his eyes started from their sockets, and he fell writhing at the officer's feet.

A R HOSSACK, Queen Victoria Rifles.

British troops wearing homemade gas masks, May 1915.

began to fatally slow down. German resistance, from isolated strongpoints, was greater than expected; local commanders' uncertainty caused delays, while inexperienced British reinforcements were slow in crossing the smashed battlefield. Above all, the breakdown of communications caused by severed telephone lines prevented the proper direction of the battle. As the British advance slowed, so the Germans recovered. Their reinforcements were not sufficiently cut up by the British guns and their own artillery had little difficulty in pinning down the British troops in their narrow bridgehead.

The battle went on for three days and although the British held on to the village they were unable to push on farther. Casualties were assessed at about 13,000 men on each side. Although a 'battle in miniature,' Neuve Chapelle demonstrated to both the French and Germans that the British Army was a force to reckon with and would play a significant role in future battles once the 'New Armies' were ready to take the field.

By early April 1915, Falkenhayn was preparing for the great Austro-German offensive in the East. To divert Allied attention and mask their real plans, the Germans launched their only attack in the West during 1915, known as the Second Battle of Ypres, in late April. The Allied defenses around Ypres consisted of the British Second Army (Smith-Dorrien) and two French divisions. The latter, holding the northern part of the salient, separated the British from the Belgian Army which was deployed along the northern section of the line.

If the German offensive came as a surprise to the Allies, the nature of the assault was an even greater shock. The Germans had experimented with poison gas on the Eastern Front earlier in 1915, but these experiments were unknown in the West and when, on the evening of 22 April, an enormous cloud began to drift slowly along the ground toward the Allied lines, it caused havoc. The dense, greenish-yellow cloud of chlorine gas was aimed at the sector of the line held by the French Algerian and Territorial divisions – low-grade formations compared with the regular French divisions. Not surprisingly, they fled in panic and British troops around Poperinghe were horrified to see African troops writhing in agony, crying out '*gaz asphyxiant!*'

By the end of the evening a dangerous gap of nearly five miles had opened up and suddenly the whole Ypres salient seemed untenable. Fortunately for the Allies, the advancing German troops were themselves reluctant to move into the gas cloud (despite their gas masks) and at a higher level the German commanders, not anticipating

LEFT: *Italian alpine infantry pose for the camera at a mountain outpost on the lower slopes of Mount Vilan.*

LEFT: Italian alpine infantry pose for the camera at a mountain outpost on the lower slopes of Mount Vilan.

RIGHT: In an even more studied pose for the camera, Italian troops adopt a fighting stance on the slopes of the Trentino shortly after Italy's declaration of war.

BELOW: An Austrian patrol trudges up a mountain path in the Alps.

BELOW RIGHT: Italian artillerymen prepare an A.13 heavy howitzer for action. In mountainous districts weapons such as the howitzer with its high elevation were essential for success in attacking prepared enemy positions.

such an early success, had failed to exploit their advantage. At the same time the Allies were again fortunate when British and Canadian reinforcements rushed forward to defend the line; during the night of the 22nd-23rd they established a string of posts to cover the gap. The cloud of poison gas was beginning to dissipate by this stage but the British Army had suffered many casualties.

The offensive carried on in earnest during the next day and what the Germans lacked in infantry reserves they made up for in the ferocity of their artillery bombardments. British frontline troops in the salient were shelled from the front and both flanks, and sometimes by German field guns in their rear – a highly unnerving experience. General Smith-Dorrien suggested a limited withdrawal, a sensible proposal but one which Sir John French (who disliked Smith-Dorrien) was to use as an excuse to sack his Second Army commander and replace him with General Sir Herbert Plumer.

Toward the end of April, Plumer ordered his men to retreat to a position similar to that suggested by Smith-Dorrien and for the next three weeks the Second Army weathered the German storm. The Germans launched successive gas, artillery and infantry assaults but the British gave only limited ground and the offensive petered out on 24 May, leaving the battered British once more in position in the Ypres salient. British casualties were high – around 60,000 men – when set against the German Army's loss of approximately 35-40,000 troops. After Second Ypres the use of gas became commonplace in the fighting on the Western Front, but the development of effective respirators rendered it more a severe irritant than a specter of mass death as had first been feared.

If May was the month of Second Ypres and the great German offensive in Galicia, it was also a month of deceptive hope for the Allies. Alone among the major European nations, Italy remained outside the war. Ever since the country's reunification in 1870 (the *Risorgimento*), Italy had nursed territorial ambitions at the expense of the Austro-Hungarian Empire. Yet Italy had been an ally of the Central Powers and even when war broke out in August 1914 she was still nominally a member of the Triple Alliance (alongside Germany and Austria). Few were surprised that Italy remained neutral and for the remainder of the year waited on the sidelines. Both Entente and Central Powers haggled for Italy's favors, but as the former could offer her the most attractive prizes in a carve-up of the Austro-Hungarian Empire, Italy declared war on Austria-Hungary on 23 May 1915. A completely opportunistic move, it was appropriately termed the *sacro egoismo* by Italian politicians.

Once the diplomatic niceties were over, the Italian Army began a series of offensives in the Alps and along the River Isonzo in the direction of Trieste, a city long desired by Italian nationalists. The inexperienced and poorly led Italian Army attacked with great dash and enthusiasm but, one by one, these offensives (a total of 11 along the Isonzo alone) failed with nothing to show but minimal gains of ground and heavy losses of men. In marked contrast to the situation on the Eastern Front, almost all the ethnic groups of the Austro-Hungarian Empire fought with fierce determination against Italy. The great complex of battles conducted along this front between 1915 and 1917 supplied some of the grimmest examples of attrition during World War I.

ABOVE LEFT: Dead German troops lie slumped in a trench, victims of a French attack during October 1915.

ABOVE: The town of Arras endures yet another bombardment.

LEFT: A French veteran walks past the ruins of a farmhouse – a common scene in frontline areas.

ABOVE RIGHT: With flags flying, a regiment of Württemberg troops marches past Crown Prince Wilhelm during a parade in the Argonne, July 1915.

RIGHT: Although carrying his Field Marshal's baton, Mackensen wears the uniform of a colonel of the Danzig Life Hussars – his old regiment.

FAR RIGHT: Orpen's The Deserter, a grim depiction of the fate that attended a soldier who quit his post during battle.

Heavy losses continued to characterize the fighting on the Western Front. May saw the resumption of the French offensives, this time in Artois under the direction of General Ferdinand Foch. This battle (Second Artois) marked a significant milestone in the war: the French used 1252 guns and howitzers, 293 of them heavy; their six-day preliminary bombardment used no fewer than 2,155,862 shells – this would be the pattern of the future. On the first day of the infantry battle (9 May) the French made a dramatic advance almost to the crest of Vimy Ridge but their reserves were too far back to exploit it. Once more, what had seemed a promising opportunity degenerated into trench attack and counterattack. The battle continued in this fashion until 18 June at a cost of over 100,000 French casualties and at least 75,000 Germans. British attempts to support the French left failed dismally due to a desperate shortage of guns (especially heavy caliber) and ammunition.

Public conern at the ammunition shortage, whipped up by the Press, led to the fall of the Liberal government, the formation of a coalition ministry and the creation of the Ministry of Munitions which, although ineffective at first, later became a valuable instrument in the conduct of the logistical side of the war.

The summer months saw a lull in the fighting while the French built up the quantities of guns and ammunition that were now essential in what had become an 'artillery war.' The knowledge that the Germans were still heavily committed in the East during September increased Joffre's confidence that a further great Allied offensive might be decisive. Champagne was again selected as the main theater of operations: a massive force of 35 divisions would be deployed for battle, while further north a 'subsidiary' offensive in Artois would dispose of 18 divisions. The artillery support was similarly massive and comprised 2000 heavy guns and 3000 field pieces.

It seemed to be an irresistible accumulation of force, and it certainly struck the Germans a heavy blow (25,000 prisoners and 150 guns were captured). But French losses

ABOVE LEFT: The two leading French generals of the war – Joffre (left) and Foch.

LEFT: An old 155mm gun is dragged into action during the offensive in Artois, May 1915.

ABOVE RIGHT: The French offensives of 1915 gained little, except row upon row of dead Frenchmen.

RIGHT: French infantry in a forward trench prepare to 'go over the top' during the offensives of June 1915.

FAR RIGHT, ABOVE: A battalion of Scottish Rifles marches up to take over new positions from the French at Laventie, August 1915.

FAR RIGHT, BELOW: French prisoners look on as German troops move up to the front line in the Argonne, 1915.

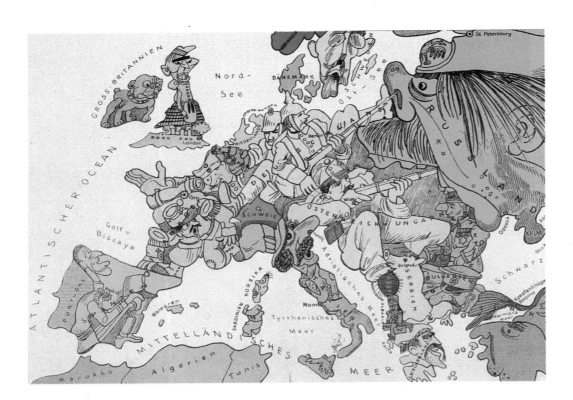

FAR LEFT: 'Maps' of this type were popular before and during the war, this is a German example by Walter Trier in 1915.

LEFT: A supposedly flattering portrait of the German Supreme War Leader, the rather stupid and vain Wilhelm II.

BELOW LEFT: Employing a captured Russian machine gun, a German team guards their strongpoint opposite French positions.

RIGHT: Kitchener reviews troops of the New Army.

BELOW: Complete with standard, French infantry launch an attack.

BELOW RIGHT: An American depiction of the 'Hun.'

Beat back the HUN with LIBERTY BONDS

F. Strothmann.

in the two offensives mounted to over 190,000 and the German lines remained unbroken. The British, attacking at Loos on the left of the French, used gas for the first time (with a notable lack of success) and were, as ever, short of artillery – only 20 heavy guns to the mile.

Whereas the French on their right failed on this occasion by having their reserves too close up so that they were caught by German artillery, the British repeated the French error of 9 May and held their reserves too far back. The result was that early gains were soon lost and the battle settled down to the all too familiar trench fighting in which losses mounted to 48,267 men. The first reserves were Kitchener Army divisions, quite inexperienced and somewhat disorganized; for them Loos was a minor disaster. There was deep dissatisfaction with the result of

Disaster at Loos

The British attack at Loos was launched in support of the major French offensive (Third Battle of Artois) of September 1915. The British forces at Loos included Regular Army and Territorial divisions as well as the first of the new divisions raised in response to Kitchener's famous call for volunteers. Poor planning, the inexperience of the troops and plain bad luck ensured that Loos was a cruel failure for the British. Great hopes had been placed on the use of gas (the first use by the British) but the wind blew in the wrong direction so that British troops were gassed instead of the enemy; the German wire remained intact and the slow-moving British troops were slaughtered in No Man's Land. The following account by a soldier in the London Irish Regiment descibes the opening of the attack (and the British habit of kicking footballs across No Man's Land):

The moment had come when it was unwise to think. The country round Loos was like a sponge; the god of war had stamped with his foot on it, and thousands of men, armed, ready to kill, were squirted out on to the level, barren fields of danger. To dwell for a moment on the novel position of standing where a thousand deaths swept by, missing you by a mere hair's breadth, would be sheer folly. There on the open field of death my life was out of my keeping, but the sensation of fear never entered my being. There was so much simplicity and so little effort in doing what I had done, in doing what 800 comrades had done, that I felt I could carry through the work before me with as much credit as my code of self-respect required. The maxims went crackle like dry brushwood under the feet of a marching host. A bullet passed very close to my face like a sharp, sudden breath; a second hit the ground in front, flicked up a little shower of dust and ricocheted to the left, hitting the earth many times before it found a resting place. The air was vicious with bullets; a million invisible birds flicked their wings very close to my face. Ahead the clouds of smoke, sluggish low-lying fog, and fumes of bursting shells, thick in volume, receded toward the German trenches, and formed a striking background for the soldiers who were marching up a low slope toward the enemy's parapet, which the smoke still hid from view. There was no haste in the forward move, every step was taken with regimental precision, and twice on the way across the Irish boys halted for a moment to correct their alignment. Only at a point on the right there was some confusion and a little irregularity. Were the men wavering? No fear! The boys on the right were dribbling the elusive football toward the German trench.

PATRICK MacGILL, London Irish Regiment.

ABOVE, FAR LEFT: *Men of the Scots Guards prime grenades (Mills bombs) in 'Big Willie' trench, October 1915.*

ABOVE LEFT: *German gunners painfully drag a massive 30.5cm heavy howitzer into position in the Argonne region. Weapons of this caliber were devastating against any target.*

FAR LEFT: *French troops relax in a frontline dugout at Ravin de Souchez, October 1915. Compared to British standards this was an almost luxurious shelter.*

LEFT: *The German equivalent – an improvised underground kitchen on the Western Front, 1915.*

Britain's largest battle so far. Field Marshal French was removed, to be succeeded as Commander in Chief of the Expeditionary Force by General Sir Douglas Haig.

1915 had proved for both sides to be a year of disappointment with success often tantalizingly close, but never within reach. On the Western Front technology was the dominant factor, a fact reflected in the increasing use of artillery and the sophistication of artillery techniques. Bombardments became more scientific with the introduction of new methods such as sound-ranging and flash-spotting, together with ever-improving communications with the aircraft that were now seen as essential for this style of war. What no one could yet see was a way of avoiding the churning up of ground in an artillery battle to such an extent that infantry and supporting guns could not move across it. Worse still, every step of technolgical progress by one side was matched by a countermove from the other. In that fact lay the frustration and tragedy of the static phase of the war.

CHAPTER FOUR

THE
WIDENING WAR

World War I began as a European war but was soon to spread across the globe. New theaters of war emerged when countries far from Europe found themselves inexorably sucked into the great conflict. This was a direct consequence of Europe's acquisition of colonial empires; it was inevitable that these territories should either supply aid – food, raw materials and manpower – to the 'mother' country or become far-flung battlegrounds. As Britain's naval supremacy was virtually worldwide in 1914, Germany had little hope of reinforcing and supplying her scattered colonial possessions, and little was expected of them. It was therefore just a matter of time before the German Empire overseas fell to the Allies, unless Germany won the war in Europe.

In the Pacific Germany controlled two groups of islands: German New Guinea and Western Samoa. Both were captured by Australian and New Zealand expeditions within a few weeks of the outbreak of war. In China, Germany leased the enclave around the port of Tsingtao, but the Japanese had their own designs on this territory. Shortly after the start of hostilities in Europe, Japan declared war on Germany (23 August) and its forces then besieged Tsingtao. Joined by a small British expeditionary force, the Japanese pressed home a major assault against the German fortifications early in November and forced a German surrender on the 7th.

Africa, however, had been the main focus of German colonial activity. By 1914 four territories lay under German rule: Togo, the Cameroons, German Southwest Africa and German East Africa. On 26 August, Togo fell to a Franco-British invasion. The campaign in the Cameroons was distinguished by stiff German resistance, but the administrative center and Duala wireless station were captured at the end of 1914. German Southwest Africa

PREVIOUS PAGES: *PREVIOUS PAGES: The war was quick to spread around the globe. Here, Japanese gunners (with a British observer) prepare a long-range naval gun for the bombardment of the isolated German garrison holding the Chinese concession port of Tsingtao. The Germans were forced to surrender on 7 November 1914.*

ABOVE LEFT: The 1st Battalion of the Nigerian Regiment entrains for action in the German Cameroons. They are armed with the old-pattern 'long' Lee Enfield rifle.

ABOVE: South African mounted troops prepare to cross the border into German Southwest Africa in support of General Botha.

LEFT: A Boer Commando photographed shortly after the outbreak of war. The declaration of war divided South Africa, and many Boers rose up against the government in a revolt that lasted until February 1915.

RIGHT: An ageing British naval 12-pounder shells enemy positions in the German Cameroons. Both sides were forced to use weapons considered grossly obsolete by Western Front standards.

presented greater problems, not least because many of the Afrikaaners of South Africa wished to reverse the decision of the Boer War. Outright rebellion broke out in South Africa during September 1914 but, although the rebels mustered some 11,000 men, their leadership was divided and after some initial successes the revolt fizzled out in February 1915. The South Africans, under the command of the famous Boer general Louis Botha (by this time Prime Minister of the Union), could only then get to grips with the Germans in Southwest Africa. Enemy strongpoints were encircled and Windhoek, the capital, fell on 12 May. On 9 July Botha accepted the German surrender; an event that marked the end of German ambitions in southern Africa.

TOP LEFT: *The Commander in Chief in German East Africa, Colonel Paul von Lettow-Vorbeck (second from right).*

TOP: *German light field artillery in action.*

ABOVE LEFT: *A consequence of the British disaster at Tanga in November 1914, captured Indian soldiers.*

ABOVE: *A German machine-gun team in action.*

LEFT: *Despite their relative newness on the colonial scene, the Germans made extensive use of their native 'Askari' troops during the campaign.*

ABOVE RIGHT: *An example of disciplined volley fire from an Askari unit.*

RIGHT: *Inhospitable terrain and harsh climatic conditions were a major problem for both sides.*

In German East Africa, the Allies faced a most formidable opponent in Lieutenant Colonel Paul von Lettow-Vorbeck. Commanding a small force (never exceeding 15,000 men and consisting chiefly of African Askaris), Lettow-Vorbeck repulsed all efforts at an invasion of the colony until February 1916 when, under the energetic leadership of General Jan Smuts, a large Allied force pushed the Germans onto the defensive. Smuts led the main body of Allied troops in a great sweep from north to south through German East Africa supported by a Belgian column advancing eastward from Lake Tanganyika, while a subsidiary British force struck from Nyasaland in the southwest. Ably exploiting the climate and terrain Lettow-Vorbeck avoided capture, although he was forced to relinquish control of the colony. Far from beaten, however, he converted his army into an irregular force and early in 1917 he slipped over the border into Portuguese Africa. There he made his base and for the remainder of the war waged a brilliant guerrilla campaign. It was only the belated news of the Armistice in Europe that led him to surrender on 23 November 1918. His achievement was made all the more remarkable by the fact that Lettow-Vorbeck kept no fewer than 372,950 British Empire troops extremely busy – British, South African, Rhodesian, Indian and African.

Despite the numbers of troops involved, the capture of Germany's colonies had little strategic significance.

Turkey's entry into the war on the side of the Central Powers in November 1914 was a different matter, however. Turkey was already heavily dependent on German economic and military aid, and her nationalistic ruling party (the 'Young Turks') cherished ambitious territorial designs against the old enemy, Russia. Germany was quick to appreciate the advantages of drawing her into the war. The Turkish Empire stretched across the Middle East and was not only a barrier to Allied reinforcement of Russia through the Black Sea, but also a threat to the Suez Canal and Britain's imperial lifelines. The Turks, enraged by the British seizure of ships built for them in British shipyards, were ready enough for war. Turkish fears of British naval might were overcome when the German battlecruiser *Goeben* and the cruiser *Breslau* sailed through the Dardanelles Straits on 10 August: the two vessels were incorporated into the Turkish Navy, their crews included. On 29 October a Turkish fleet which included these two ships bombarded Russian ports in the Black Sea; on 1 November Russia declared war on Turkey, joined four days later by France and Britain.

Turkey's first military act was a long-planned expedition into the Russian Caucasus to threaten the Baku oilfields. Under the command of Turkey's leader, Enver Pasha the assault was launched on 22 December 1914. The Turkish Army was unprepared for the harsh conditions of a Caucasian winter, however, and on 1 January

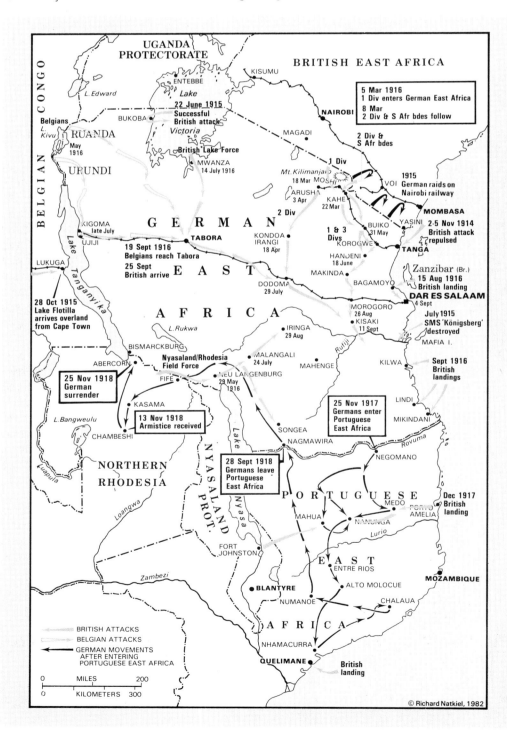

1915 was severely defeated by the Russians at Sarikamish in a four-day battle which left only 18,000 Turkish survivors from an original force of 95,000 men. This marked the end of the Turkish offensive against Russia, although fighting continued in a desultory fashion over the next two years of the war.

The failure of the Turkish campaign had the unfortunate effect of increasing Turkish hostility toward the Christian population within the province of Armenia close to the Russian frontier. Relations between the two religious groups were poor and the Armenians had been maltreated by their more powerful Moslem neighbors for generations. Once war broke out the Armenians were seen to be in league with the Russians and, following the Turkish defeat at Sarikamish, Moslem hatred rose to fever pitch. Violent attacks by Turkish vigilante groups increased and, when on 11 June 1915, the Turkish Government began a policy of widespread deportation, atrocities occurred on a massive scale. Accurate figures of the extent of this policy of virtual genocide are hard to arrive at, but estimates of over a million deaths seem realistic. Although these deaths were not particularly unusual by the standards of the war, such barbaric behavior nevertheless caused universal horror and revulsion when news of the massacres filtered out. Tragically, this episode proved to be a portent of things to come in the next war.

Early in 1915 the Turks had made a number of raids on the Suez Canal from Palestine, and although they were easily repelled by the defending British and Empire troops, this threat to Britain's 'jugular vein' was taken seriously. A large British garrison was stationed in Egypt – at one point rising to over 250,000 men – and was effectively tied down by the Turks, who skilfully deployed a small force in Sinai to threaten the canal and also sent agents to foment 'trouble' from the Sensussi tribesmen in Egypt's Western Desert.

In 1916 the British went on the offensive. In June of that year the Sherif of Mecca organized a revolt against Turkish rule in Arabia. This coincided with a slow British advance along the Mediterranean coast of Sinai. Under the command of General Sir Archibald Murray the British painstakingly laid a railway and water pipeline across the desert, and it was only at the end of the 1916 that El Arish was occupied and an assault on Turkish Palestine became a practical military possibility.

Turkey's entry into the war seemed to offer an opportunity for sea power – in particular British naval supremacy – to supply the desired alternative to the trench deadlock on the Western Front. British thinking hardened steadily upon an expedition to the Dardanelles, aimed at gaining control of Constantinople and the Bosporus. The goal was to open an ice-free route to Russia through which she could export her grain surplus and import much-needed munitions. At first it was believed that the Royal Navy could carry out such a project without army support. Heavy losses of old French and British battleships to Turkish mines in the Narrows, however, prompted a call for a military back-up expedition.

The problem was finding the men. By late April a mixed force of British regulars, a naval division, ANZACs (the Australian and New Zealand Army Corps) and French troops were assembled in Egypt under General Sir Ian Hamilton. Their objective was to attack the Dardanelles and occupy the Gallipoli Peninsula. With the Canadians heavily engaged at Ypres and the South Africans fighting in Southwest Africa, the participation of Australians and New Zealanders at Gallipoli confirmed the unique contribution of the British self-governing Dominions to the war.

The southernmost tip of the Gallipoli Peninsula was selected as the site for the main landings which would take place on five beaches. Ten miles further north a secondary landing would be made, this being the responsibility of the ANZACs. The troops went ashore on 25 April and immediately ran into problems. The strong currents ensured that some landing parties arrived on the wrong beaches, a situation which, along with poor maps and unfamiliar, difficult terrain, led to confusion and delay. Most of the landings met fierce Turkish resistance and, lacking special equipment for amphibious operations, the attacking forces suffered heavily. The assault was conducted with the utmost bravery but the dash of the attackers was met by an equally tenacious defense, and the natural balance of material forces being with the defenders meant the Allies were only able to secure the most tenuous footholds at Cape Hellas and Anzac Cove.

ABOVE: The British Commander in Chief at Gallipoli, General Sir Ian Hamilton (left), leading the cheers of his officers during an award ceremony.

LEFT: SS River Clyde, the troopship that was run aground on one of the beaches at Cape Hellas.

BELOW: General Liman von Sanders, the able German commander of the Turkish forces at Gallipoli.

RIGHT: *A trench scene at Anzac Cove – men of the Royal Naval Division and ANZACs look through periscopes toward the Turkish positions. This section of line later became known as Quinn's and Courtney's Posts. It was at Gallipoli that the ANZACs established their reputation as first-class fighting troops.*

ABOVE LEFT: *Turkish dead lie sprawled across No Man's Land.*

BELOW: *Desperately short of trench weapons, the Allies in the Middle East were forced to improvise, as here where men are constructing homemade grenades from empty tins.*

BOTTOM: *Australian troops prepare for action in a support trench near Quinn's Post during the attack on 25 May 1915.*

Gallipoli Armistice

The trench fighting between the Turks and the British and ANZACs was among the most brutal of the whole war. Each side fought with the utmost resolution and casualties were high. Occasionally, truces were called for the retrieval and burial of the dead in No Man's Land. The Honorable Aubrey Herbert was an officer on the British side responsible for organizing one of these truces:

We mounted over a plateau and down through gullies filled with thyme where there lay about 4000 Turkish dead. It was indescribable. One was grateful for the rain and the grey sky . . . There were two wounded crying in that multitude of silence . . . The Turkish captain with me said: 'At this spectacle even the most gentle must feel savage, and the most savage must weep.' The dead fill acres of ground, mostly killed in the one big attack, but some recently. They fill the myrtle-grown gullies. One saw the result of machine-gun fire very clearly: entire companies annihilated – not wounded, but killed, their heads doubled under them with the impetus of their rush and both hands clasping their bayonets. It was as if God had breathed in their faces . . .

A good deal of friction at first. The trenches were 10 to 15 yards apart. Each side was on the *qui vive* for treachery. In one gully the dead got to be left unburied. It was impossible to bury them without one side seeing the position of the other. In the Turkish parapet there were many bodies buried. Fahreddin told Skeen he wanted to bury them. 'But,' he said, 'we cannot take them out without putting something in their place.'

I talked to the Turks, one of whom pointed to the graves. 'That's politics,' he said. Then he pointed to the dead bodies and said, 'That's diplomacy. God pity all of us poor soldiers.'

. . . At four o'clock the Turks came to me for orders. I do not believe this could have happened anywhere else. I retired their troops and ours, walking along the line. At 0407 hours I retired the white-flag men, making them shake hands with our men. Then I came to the upper end. About a dozen Turks came out. I chaffed them, and said they would shoot me next day. They said, in a horrified chorus: 'God forbid!' The Albanians laughed and cheered, and said: 'We will never shoot you.' Then the Australians began coming up, and said: 'Good-bye, old chap; good luck!' And the Turks said: 'Oghur ola gule gule gedejekseniz, gule gule gelejekseniz' (Smiling may you go and smiling come again). Then I told them all to get into their trenches, and unthinkingly went up to the Turkish trench and got a deep salaam from it.

THE HONORABLE AUBREY HERBERT

The Kiwi Stoics

Although the bitter battles on the Gallipoli Peninsula continued for months on end, the Allied soldiers' will to fight on never diminished, as this account testifies:

The troops quartered in this fort were an Indian Field Battery and 63 New Zealanders, all that was left of their battalion. These men had been in the first landing. They had had, every one of them, dysentery or fever, and the great majority were still sick and overripe for hospital.

As time went on, and illness increased, one often heard men and officers say: 'If we can't hold the trenches with sound men, we have got to hold them with sick men.' When all was quiet, the sicklist grew daily. But when the men knew that there was to be an attack, they fought their sickness to fight the Turk, and the stream to the hospitals shrank.

I admired nothing in the war more than the spirit of these 63 New Zealanders, who were soon to go to their last fight. When the day's work was over and the sunset swept the sea, we used to lean upon the parapet and look up to where Chunuk Bahr flamed, and

talk. The great distance from their own country created an atmosphere of loneliness. This loneliness was emphasized by the fact that the New Zealanders rarely received the same recognition as the Australians in the Press, and many of their gallant deeds went unrecorded or were attributed to their greater neighbors. But they had a silent pride that put these things into proper perspective. The spirit of these men was unconquered and unconquerable. At night, when the great moon of the Dardanelles soared, and all was quiet except the occasional whine of a bullet overhead, the voices of the tired men continually argued the merits of the expedition, and there was always one end to these discussions: 'Well, it may all be a ——— mistake, but in a war this size you will have mistakes of this size, and it doesn't matter a ——— to us whether we are for it here or in France, for we came out to do one job, and it's nothing to us whether we finish in one place or another.' The Turks were not the only fatalists in those days . . .

THE HONORABLE AUBREY HERBERT.

Once the whereabouts of the landings became known to the Turkish command – ably directed by the German military adviser, General Liman von Sanders – counter-attacks were launched. The Turks flung themselves with the utmost ferocity at the hastily dug Allied trenches, but were unable to dislodge the invaders. Trench warfare stalemate, similar to that of the Western Front, was once again the result.

The enclosed space of the battlefield, which consisted of a succession of rocky gullies and ridges, and the extreme climate provided Gallipoli with its unique hellish character. For the Allies shortages of ammunition and supplies, including water, made the situation critical, while conditions for the troops were rendered almost unbearable by the inevitable outbreak of disease. Regular and widespread attacks of dysentery – an examination of seven Australian battalions found 78 percent of the men suffering from the disease – seriously sapped the troops' strength and morale.

In order to resolve the deadlock, reinforcements were sent out to Hamilton and new landings were proposed farther north on the Gallipoli Peninsula. Unfortunately for the British, most of these reinforcements were inexperienced soldiers led by ageing officers whose leadership abilities were found sorely wanting. The new landings were made at Suvla Bay on 6 August, while the ANZACs launched a diversionary operation from Anzac Cove a few miles south of the main operation. Amazingly, the attackers encountered almost no resistance at Suvla Bay, but instead of pressing on they allowed the surprised Turks to regroup and bring up reinforcements to confine the attackers to yet another beach-head. A golden opportunity had been lost and trench deadlock was resumed.

RIGHT: *Part of the great evacuation from Gallipoli, December 1915. A field gun and limber are transported from Saval Point on rafts. The Dardanelles was one of the most heartbreaking of all the campaigns fought by the British and Dominion forces.*

BELOW LEFT: *A typically spirited Australian bayonet charge at Anzac Cove, December 1915.*

BELOW: *Horses stand picketed on the beach road made between Cape Hellas and Gully Ravine. The close proximity of Allied positions on the peninsula to Turkish artillery ensured that there were no real rear areas and all but the most sheltered gullies were vulnerable to high-angle fire.*

The steadily mounting casualty list and the frustrating lack of success led to demands for abandoning the whole venture. Hamilton was recalled on 16 October and his successor, General Sir Hector Monro, recommended withdrawal, a view endorsed by Kitchener himself following a tour of inspection. During December and January skillfully conducted evacuations of the beach-head were carried out, marking a sad end to a brave endeavor. The forces of the British Empire suffered a total of 213,980 casualties (114,649 in battle), the French 47,000 and the Turks at least 251,000, although some estimates place this figure at nearer 350,000.

The 1915 British campaign in Mesopotamia began as a simple operation to safeguard oil installations in the Persian Gulf but weak Turkish resistance along the River Tigris encouraged an advance farther inland. One of the more distinguishing characteristics of the campaign was the almost complete lack of political control from London. No clear objective was set, save that the capture of Baghdad might be a good idea, and the ambitions of the soldiers on the spot were allowed full rein. Under the command of General Sir John Nixon, a scratch force was gathered together, the main element being three brigades of infantry from the Indian Army (each containing one British and three Indian battalions). The occupation of Basra had been effected with only token Turkish resistance and, although there were good military reasons for calling a halt to the expedition at this point, it was decided to press on. The complete failure of a Turkish counterattack in April only encouraged Nixon in this scheme.

Major General Charles Townshend was appointed to command the river-borne expedition up the Tigris, dispatched early in May. Turkish resistance was minimal, although progress was slow due to logistical problems. The Mesopotamian climate is one of the most extreme in the world and the wealth of dangerous diseases encountered by the British soon overwhelmed the pitifully small medical services at their disposal. Like many such poorly planned ventures, the support services were woefully inadequate. Despite this, the city of Kut-al-Amara was

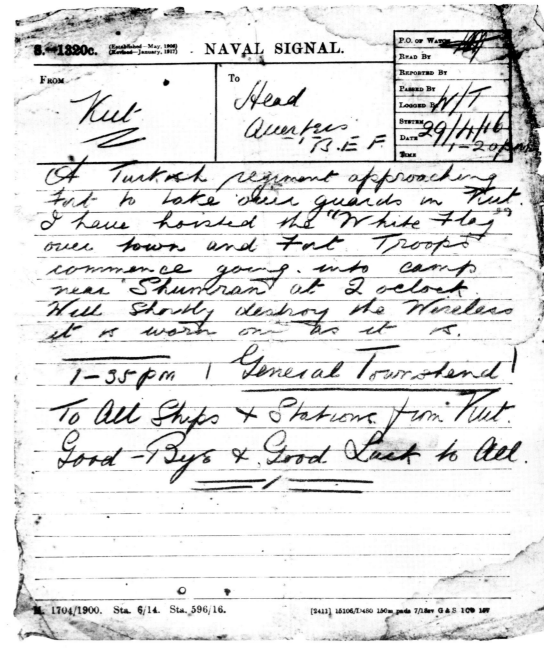

LEFT: *The doleful signal from General Townshend announcing the end of British resistance at Kut represented Britain's greatest military disaster of the war.*

BELOW, FAR LEFT: *Major General Charles Townshend, leader of the ill-fated British expedition up the River Tigris.*

BELOW LEFT: *Turkish treatment of the British and Empire forces taken at Kut was generally of the worst kind, as evidenced by these exchanged Indian prisoners suffering from severe malnutrition.*

ABOVE RIGHT: *Indian troops are landed on the right bank of the Tigris, a short distance from the firing line. River boats of this sort were, however, in short supply.*

RIGHT: *Many attempts were made to relieve Townshend's garrison at Kut and included airdrops of food by BE2's of No. 30 Squadron. Although highly innovative, the capacity of such aircraft was severely limited, as was their overall effect in attempting to break the siege.*

BELOW RIGHT: *The famous arch of Ctesiphon, the high-water mark of Townshend's adventure.*

The Mesopotamian Adventure

Among the many shortcomings of leadership and planning that accompanied Townshend's advance up the Tigris was the inadequate provision for the sick and wounded. An army doctor, Major R Markham Carter, wrote this report of the awful conditions encountered in this theater of operations:

I was standing on the bridge in the evening when the *Medjidieh* arrived. She had two steel barges, without any protection against the rain as far as I remember. As this ship with its two barges came up to us I saw that she was absolutely packed, and the barges too, with men. The barges were slipped and the *Medjidieh* was brought alongside the *Varela*. When she was about 300 or 400 yards off it looked as if she was festooned with ropes. The stench when she was close was quite definite, and I found that what I mistook for ropes were dried stalactites of human faeces. The patients were so huddled and crowded together on the ship that they could not perform the offices of nature clear of the edge of the ship, and the whole of the ship's side was covered with stalactites of human faeces. This is what I then saw. A certain number of men were standing and kneeling on the immediate perimeter of the ship. Then we found a mass of men huddled up anyhow – some with blankets and some without. They were lying in a pool of dysentery about 30 feet square. They were covered with dysentery and dejecta generally from head to foot. With regard to the first man I examined, I put my hand into his trousers, and I thought that he had a haemorrhage. His trousers were full almost to the waist with something warm and slimy. I took my hand out and thought it was a blood clot. It was dysentery. The men had a fractured thigh, and his thigh was perforated in five or six places. He had apparently been writhing about the deck of the ship. Many cases were almost as bad. There were a certain number of cases of terribly bad bedsores. In my report I describe mercilessly to the Government of India how I found men with their limbs splinted with wood strips from Johnny Walker whisky boxes, 'Bhoosa' wire, and that sort of thing.

MAJOR R MARKHAM CARTER.

taken on 28 September and the overambitious Townshend began to make preparations for an advance on Baghdad. As the British marched farther up the Tigris their strength declined, while that of the Turks increased. Outside Ctesiphon (16 miles from Baghdad) the Turks made their stand – 20,000 men against the 12,000 troops of Townshend.

In a confused engagement the Turks held their ground and, increasingly isolated, Townshend was forced to fall back to Kut. Even at this point British action was characterized by a general sense of complacency and, when a reinforced Turkish army began to besiege Kut, the British soon found themselves in severe difficulty. As the siege wore on desperate attempts were made to relieve the beleaguered defenders, but every attempt to send troops up the Tigris to Kut was thwarted. A number of aircraft were gathered to drop supplies from the air, but were obviously

too few in number to help the garrison which by the end of the year was beginning to starve. Conditions worsened progressively and, with no hope of relief, Townshend surrendered to the Turks on 29 April 1916. The loss of Kut was the greatest British military disaster of the war and did much to further the Turkish cause in the Middle East at the expense of British influence.

Turkey, although a secondary enemy, had proved a far tougher opponent than the British had anticipated and the campaigns in the Middle East were a significant drain on British resources. In the course of the war some 2,500,000 British and Empire troops were sucked into the Middle East conflict, yet none of these campaigns was to have any serious effect on the main war against Germany. Perhaps worst of all was the palpable failure of sea power to resolve the strategic impasse, thus committing Britain to making her main effort as a land power.

In addition the Allied expedition to Salonika caused the Germans no serious embarrassment. In December 1915 an offensive was launched to strike northward against Bulgaria, but this came to nothing and the Allied troops fell back to Salonika. Reinforced by the refugee Serbs, now reorganized and re-equipped, Italians and contingents from Gallipoli, the force at Salonika grew to a strength of over 600,000 men by 1917. German observers of this great diversion of Allied strength from the main theaters of war sardonically described Salonika as the 'greatest Allied internment camp' of the conflict. It was a conspicuous example of the Allied tendency toward dispersal of effort and contrasted sharply with Germany's economical use of small military contingents in support of her allies. Small teams of advisers were dispatched to key areas where their experience could be best used without draining German resources on the Western Front. This judicious distribution of German weapons, munitions, personnel and economic aid helped to keep her weaker partners in the field for much of the war.

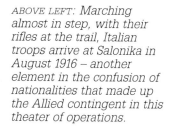

ABOVE LEFT: Marching almost in step, with their rifles at the trail, Italian troops arrive at Salonika in August 1916 – another element in the confusion of nationalities that made up the Allied contingent in this theater of operations.

LEFT: A Serbian artillery battery in action on the Macedonian Front. The Serbs, largely re-equipped by the French, were arguably the most effective fighting force available to the Allies in Salonika.

ABOVE RIGHT: Despite their French Adrian-pattern steel helmets, these are Russian troops marching toward the front line following their arrival in Salonika.

RIGHT: A British 18-pounder in action, November 1916. The British contingent occupied the right of the Allied line and faced the Bulgarian Army which they found to be a redoubtable opponent.

CHAPTER FIVE

STALEMATE & SLAUGHTER

Throughout 1915 the Central Powers had one great strategic advantage – the ability to wage war on interior lines – and they put it to good use. Their strategic railways enabled them to transfer forces swiftly from front to front. The Allies had no such facility; thus, while the Germans could move 24 divisions from west to east in a month, it took four months to transport just nine divisions from France to Egypt and vice versa. In the face of such overwhelming difficulty the Allies, under General Joffre's guidance, were nevertheless slowly working toward a strategy of simultaneous offensives against the Central Powers. The Inter-Allied Military Conference at Chantilly, held in December 1915, formulated the Allies' broad strategic plan for 1916: concentric military, naval and economic pressure to crush Germany and her confederates of which the central feature would be a decisive French attack with strong British support.

In February 1916, however, Germany passed to the offensive in the West. General Falkenhayn planned a mortal blow against the French Army, weakened by almost 2,000,000 casualties since the war began. Falkenhayn had successfully argued against other colleagues who favored further offensives in the East in 1916 or an assault on Italy. Falkenhayn was concerned that further Allied offensives in the West might have serious consequences on German morale, while an offensive would blunt an Allied assault. Moreover, he now regarded Britain as Germany's main enemy and, having been refused unrestricted submarine warfare (the most suitable weapon to bring Britain to its knees), Falkenhayn turned to a conventional land campaign. Rather than attack the British directly, however, he decided to strike a blow against France, described by him as 'Britain's best sword.' With Russia seemingly crippled by the 1915 disaster, England would be fatally isolated if France could be knocked out of the war.

Trainloads of German troops were transported from the East to the Western Front and, with a reserve of more than 25 divisions plus considerably superior heavy artillery, prospects augured well. This time, the usual hope of a strategic breakthrough was exchanged for the prospect of 'bleeding France to death' by attacking a particular sector of the French line which they would feel compelled to defend regardless of loss. This was the true beginning of undisguised attritional warfare.

The salient around the fortress of Verdun was chosen as the killing ground. Not only was it of strong emotional value to the French, it also allowed the Germans to bring the maximum amount of heavy artillery to bear on the defenders. Artillery was the cornerstone of the tactical plan. Limited assaults by the infantry would seize key points in order to draw in French reserves for grinding in the 'mill' of the German guns. The German Fifth Army under the command of the Kaiser's eldest son, Crown Prince Wilhelm, was to attack Verdun. Six infantry divisions (with three in reserve) were in position along a front of eight miles supported by an array of more than 1200 artillery pieces, nearly half of which were of heavy caliber. The assault force was concealed behind the front line with utmost secrecy. Reports of a German build-up were disregarded by the French High Command which designated Verdun as a quiet sector and had stripped the forts of heavy artillery to supply the active field armies.

Just after 0700 hours on 21 February 1916 the Germans opened their bombardment of the French positions, the barrage was the most devastating yet experienced in warfare. During the afternoon of the 21st groups of German infantry advanced toward the shattered French frontline trenches. Despite the ferocity of their bombardment, the Germans were surprised to find pockets of French troops holding on. The scale of the artillery assault had convinced the German commanders – as it convinced the British on the Somme a few months later – that their infantry would only be called upon actually to take

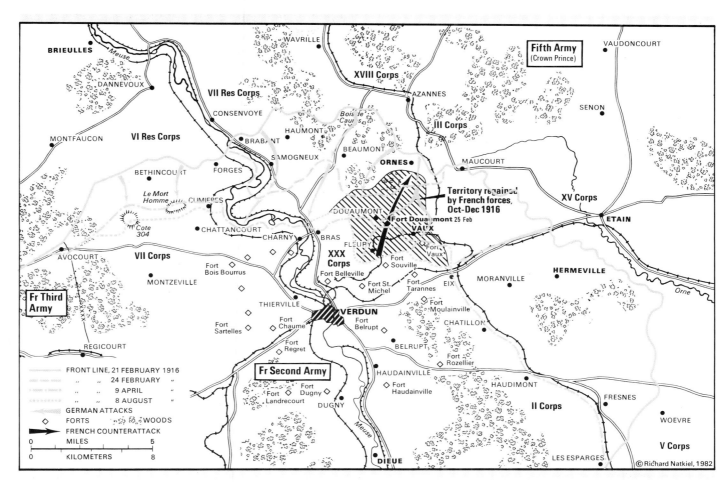

PREVIOUS PAGES: A scene from the Battle of the Somme – British and German wounded make their way to a dressing station.

ABOVE: General Philippe Pétain, the 'Savior of Verdun.'

LEFT: A German heavy howitzer blasts away at French entrenchments.

CENTER LEFT: French troops prepare a mortar while awaiting a German attack.

BELOW LEFT: The confined battlefield of Verdun and the length of the battle – from 21 February to 18 December 1916 – gave the struggle a special horror as exemplified by this corpse.

RIGHT: The Battle of Verdun.

BELOW: A scene from the early stages of the Verdun battle – German assault troops move past their own chevaux de frise.

physical possession of the battered enemy trenches. To their consternation, groups of French troops survived the barrage and refused either to retreat or surrender. Such resolute defense broke the cohesion of the German attack, thereby preventing any tactical breakthrough. For such resistance the defenders paid a high price. For example, in the first few days of fighting a regiment led by the redoubtable Colonel Driant suffered 1800 casualties from an effective strength of just 2000 men.

The Germans pressed forward and on 25 February the French line began to waver. A colonial division defending the slopes around the key position of Fort Douaumont broke and fled before a concerted German attack. Worse was to follow when a small patrol of German pioneers captured the largely intact Fort Douaumont itself which, through a glaring oversight, was defended by a few second-grade Territorial troops. These setbacks caused a crisis in French morale and there was talk of abandoning

The Treatment of Casualties

World War I was the first war in which serious provision for the wounded was made. Advances in medical science during the nineteenth century ensured that many wounds could be successfully treated. Although the development of an efficient system for the collection and treatment of the wounded was equally important.

Once a soldier was injured he usually dropped out of battle. If possible he would walk back for medical attention – a member of 'the walking wounded.' Those more badly hurt would lie where they fell, hoping to be picked up by regimental stretcher-bearers. A wounded man would receive his first treatment at the regimental aid post, normally situated within the trench lines themselves, where proper dressings would be applied, morphine injections given when necessary and where a general assessment of the man's condition would be made by the regimental medical officer. Light wounds could be dealt with here, but anything more serious was sent down the line to the Casualty Clearing Station (CCS), usually sited a few miles behind the line with a staff of 100 or more people capable of carrying out all forms of basic surgery. The CCS was the key link in the whole medical chain. The onset of infection was

the biggest danger facing a wounded soldier: if he could receive appropriate treatment at a CCS within 24-30 hours, he would most likely survive the horrors of gangrene and other fatal infections. After treatment at the CCS the patient would usually be sent to a hospital in the rear for further treatment or convalescence.

The scale of casualties in World War I exceeded all but the wildest speculation and the medical services expanded to meet the demand. The British Royal Army Medical Corps entered the war with a personnel strength of 20,000 but by 1918 this had risen to 150,000, supplemented by tens of thousands of volunteers from the Red Cross and other charities. The treatment of the wounded was one of the ironic success stories of the war, at least for the British, Americans and, in the main, the Germans.

Other countries failed to cope with the massive problem of millions of wounded men. Not surprisingly, the medical services of the less well-developed nations – Russia, Austria-Hungary, Turkey, for example – collapsed under the strain, but France too had a poor medical record. Interestingly, the old military adage that good medical care is the best tonic for morale held true in World War I.

The exhausted French garrison of Fort Vaux.

the right bank of the Meuse to the Germans. However, Joffre's deputy, General de Castelnau, arrived at Verdun on the 25th and decided to hang on to the right bank, regardless of increasing German pressure and rapidly growing casualties.

It was at this stage that General Henri Philippe Pétain arrived as commander of the Second Army defending Verdun. An excellent tactician, Pétain had gained a reputation as a general who cared for his men. He immediately set about organizing the supply, reinforcement and relief of his hard-pressed troops. The road from Bar-le-Duc was the only route into Verdun not under German artillery fire – a vital artery which was called *La Voie Sacrée* ('the Sacred Way'). Along it 3000 lorries a day transported the men,

TOP: *A German soldier takes aim from a shell-smashed trench while alongside him a French corpse 'returns to the soil.'*

ABOVE: *A French bayonet charge across No Man's Land. The ferocity of French counterattacks came as a shock to the commanders of German Fifth Army.*

LEFT: *French troops rest alongside La Voie Sacrée, upon which can be seen motorized trucks stretching to the horizon, 8 April 1916.*

FAR RIGHT: *A German sentry uses a periscope to survey No Man's Land.*

TOP RIGHT: *The extraordinary devastation of the Verdun battlefield can be guessed at from this aerial photograph of Fort Vaux taken in August 1916.*

ABOVE RIGHT: *Using a captured German Maxim machine gun, French infantrymen fire at German troops around Fort Douaumont, scene of an early French disaster.*

RIGHT: *Occupying a trench made from shell craters and foxholes, a French forward detachment has moved into No Man's Land in an attempt to push the French line forward toward the German positions around Fort Douaumont.*

weapons, ammunition and stores that kept Verdun alive. At the height of the battle, lorries traveled at the rate of one every 14 seconds and a division's worth of Territorial troops were engaged in keeping the road open. Repairs were carried out immediately with materials gathered from a nearby quarry; broken down vehicles were simply manhandled into the ditch.

German casualties at Verdun steadily mounted in the face of the Second Army's increasing artillery fire and skillfully mounted counterattacks. Throughout March, April and May the battle raged with undiminished intensity; if the French were being put through the mill, so too were the Germans. Falkenhayn had given the Crown Prince permission to extend the width of the assault, and during April and May the Germans waged bitter battles for possession of the hills and ridges on the east bank of the Meuse. Much of the fighting was concentrated around the aptly named spur of *Mort Homme* ('Dead Man'). For the troops of both sides the 'Hell of Verdun' was a way of life. By the end of April 42 French divisions had been through Verdun while the corresponding German figure was 30, a reflection of the opposing systems: the French rotated formations regularly, the Germans tended to hold them in place until completely exhausted and unfit for fighting.

The Germans continued with their advance and gained some successes, though in the end these were to prove illusory. After a succession of assaults the Germans took Fort Vaux on 7 June, following a heroic defense by an infantry battalion under Major Sylvain-Eugène Raynal. The troops in Fort Vaux had withstood repeated artillery assaults and, once the Germans had captured the outer superstructure, they also endured the horrors of flame-

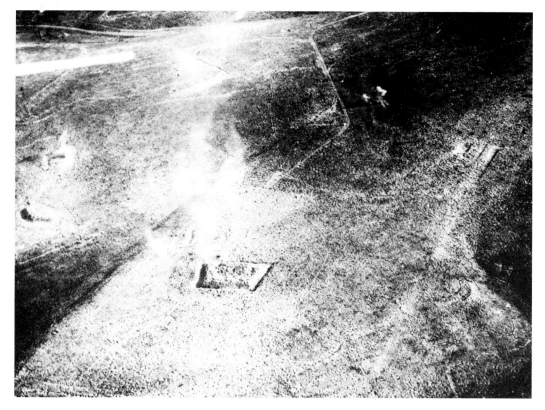

The Fight for Fort Vaux

Although recovering from his third wound at the front the 49-year-old Commandant Raynal answered the call for a volunteer to take command of the key position of Fort Vaux in the Verdun defenses. Raynal kept a journal of his epic struggle to hold the key position, from which the following extracts are taken:

So we came to 4 June, a day still more terrible. About 8.30am, the Boches carried out two attacks in combination: one against the barricade of the observation post: the other on the barricade of the left arches. Through the loopholes, they poured flame and gas which gave off an intolerable smell and gripped our throats. Shouts of 'gas masks' came from both ends of the fort. In the left arches, the garrison, driven back by flame and smoke, fell back toward the central gallery. Here was posted brave Lieutenant Girard. He dashed forward into the smoke to the machine guns which his men had been forced to abandon. He had the luck to get there before the Boches, and at once opened fire on the sheet of gas which was pouring through the right-hand barricade. Inspired by his example, his men came back, stood to their guns and fired for an hour without stopping. After clearing the ground between the machine guns and the barricade, Girard led forward the bombers who reoccupied their position and definitely drove the Boche off. In this bitter engagement, fought out in the midst of smoke and complete darkness (for the gas had put out all the lamps), Girard received several bits of bomb in his face and hands; fortunately slight wounds. He did not go back to the casemate of Bourges-Left until the position had been completely re-established. But on reaching it, he was seized with violent sickness from the gas he had swallowed and fainted. Under the care that was taken of him, he revived and at once took over his sector.

It was in the course of that afternoon that the sapper sergeant in charge of the stores came and asked to speak to me in private, and said in a hoarse voice: 'Mon commandant, there is practically no water left in the cistern.' I started, I made him repeat what he had said. I shook him. 'There has been dirty work here.' 'No sir, we have only served out the ration you laid down. It is the marks on the register which have been wrong.' Then our agony began. I gave orders to hold back the little that remained and to make no further allowances today . . .

During this day, 6 June, the Boche became more active against our barricades. It was as if he guessed the drama which was being played out within, and in actual fact the sufferings of my men, above all of the wounded, increased terribly. Thirst, that horrible thirst, raged. It was the end. Unless a miracle happened, this would be the last night of our resistance. My men, who drank no more, ate no more, slept no longer, only held themselves upright by a prodigy of will.

I summoned my officers to my command post. Every one of these brave men now despaired. They saw no salvation for their men, who must be preserved for the sake of the country, except by immediate surrender. But suddenly the guns outside began to bark, and the barking grew to a tempest. They were French guns. The fort was not being touched, but the vicinity was being violently barraged. The flame of hope once more sprang up. 'Listen, comrades. That is French artillery. It has never fired so strongly. It is the preparation for an attack. Go to your positions. Tomorrow morning, if we have not been delivered, I promise to submit to cruel necessity.'

Warmed by my words, the officers returned to their posts. About 11pm our gunfire abruptly ceased and the night passed away in complete calm, more nerve-racking for me than the storm of battle. Not a sound, not a hint of movement. I thought of the promise I had made. Had I the right to prolong resistance beyond human strength and to compromise uselessly the life of these brave men who had done their duty so heroically? I took a turn in the corridors. What I saw was frightening. Men overcome with vomiting due to urine in the stomach, for so wretched were they that they had reached the point of drinking their own urine. Some lost consciousness. In the main gallery, a man was licking a little wet streak on the wall . . .

7 June! Day broke, and we scarcely noticed it. For us it was still night, a night in which all hope was extinguished. Aid from outside, if it came, would come too late. I sent off my last message, the last salute of the fort and its defenders to their country. Then I turned to my men: 'It is all over, my friends. You have done your duty, the whole of your duty. Thank you.' They understood, and together in one shout we repeated the last message which my instrument had just sent off: 'Vive la France!' In the minutes which followed a silence as of death fell upon the fort.

throwers and gas squirted through crevices in the fort. Only when the water supply failed – the men were reduced to drinking their own urine – did Raynal surrender. The Crown Prince was sufficiently impressed to honor his captive by ceremonially returning Raynal his sword.

The French began to waver again in June, but Joffre urged his commanders to hang on for a little longer, knowing that the imminent Somme offensive would take the pressure off the exhausted defenders. Thus Pétain's request made on 23 June to evacuate his forces to the left bank of the Meuse was refused. The battle raged on but the French managed to hold their ground – just. On 1 July the long-awaited Allied offensive on the Somme opened. German reinforcements were re-routed away from Verdun and Falkenhayn closed down the offensive against the French on the 11th.

From the end of July, the French went over to the offensive and in a series of ferocious counterattacks regained much of the ground they had lost in the early stages of the battle. Pétain had been replaced by General Robert Nivelle who, like General Foch, was an apostle of the offensive. On 24 October and 15 December Nivelle launched two major assaults on the German positions. They came to be regarded as definitive models of the limited offensive. Massive artillery support and well-defined and realistic objectives characterized these attacks. The German positions were poor. Their rear areas consisted of a shell-racked crater-zone up to eight miles deep, making communication and supply a nightmare for them. The first attack recaptured Fort Douaumont and took 6000 prisoners, while the second pushed the Germans back two miles and yielded a further 11,000 prisoners plus 115 guns. French artillery techniques had improved enormously since the futile offensives of 1915. Nivelle's star rose accordingly.

On 18 December a final and highly successful French

RIGHT: French troops inspect the main outer walls of Fort Vaux in early June 1916. They are in reasonably good condition despite the attentions of German heavy artillery.

ABOVE RIGHT: A group of three French veterans from a colonial regiment take a rest amid the devastation of Verdun.

FAR RIGHT: Another Verdun scene of French troops resting between attacks. Soldiers were able to snatch a few hours sleep almost regardless of external conditions.

The First Day of the Battle of the Somme

A disaster with few parallels, the First Day of the Somme has achieved a special notoriety in British military annals. No army in modern history suffered so many casualties in so short a space of time, and yet to the British Army's great credit, the battle was resumed the next day and carried on until 13 November 1916. By the end the British had outfought the German Army, the most professional army in Europe, the yardstick against which other forces were judged. The following extract is from an account written by an NCO of the 22nd Manchester Rifles (7th Pals), a battalion from the famous 7th Division, which was involved in the attack between the two villages of Fricourt and Marne on 1 July 1916 and tells of the opening of the battle:

It was the last hour of the bombard-ment – at least, I mean, before we went over the top – and, as though there were some mysterious sympathy be-tween the wonders of the ear and the eye, that bewildering tumult seemed to grow more insistent with the growing brilliance of the atmosphere and the intenser blue of the July sky. The sound was different, not only in magni-tude but in quality, from anything known to me. It was not a succession of explosions or a continuous roar: I, at least, never heard either a gun or a bursting shell. It was not a noise; it was a symphony. And it did not move. It hung over us. It seemed as though the air was full of a vast and agonized pas-sion, bursting now with groans and sighs, now into shrill screaming and pitiful whimpering, shuddering beneath terrible blows, torn by unearthly whips, vibrating with the solemn pulses of enormous wings.

At 7.30am we went up the ladders, doubled through the gaps in the wire and lay down, waiting for the line to form up on each side of us. When it was ready, we went forward, not doubling,

but at a walk. For we had 900 yards of rough ground to the trench which was our first objective, and about 1500 yards to a further trench where we were to wait for orders.

I had been worried by the thoughts: 'Suppose one should lose one's head and get other men cut up! Suppose one's legs should take fright and refuse to move!' Now I knew it was all right. I shouldn't be frightened and I shouldn't lose my head. Just imagine the joy of that discovery! I felt quite happy and self-possessed. It wasn't courage. That, I imagine, is the quality of facing danger which one knows to be danger, of making one's spirit triumph over the bestial desire to live in this body. But I knew that I was in no danger.

In crossing No Man's Land we must have lost more men than I realized then. For the moment, the sight of the Germans drove everything else out of my head. Most men, I suppose, have a paleolithic savage somewhere in them, a beast that occasionally shouts to be given a chance of showing his joyful cunning in destruction. I have anyway, and from the age of catapults to that of shotguns have always enjoyed aiming at anything that moved, though since manhood the pleasure has been sneaking and shame-faced. Now it was a duty to shoot, and there was a splen-did target. For the Germans were brave men, idiotically brave. They actually knelt, even stood, on the top of their parapet, within less than 150 yards of us. It was insane. One couldn't miss them. Every man I fired at dropped except one. Him, the boldest of the lot, I missed repeatedly. I was puzzled and angry. Two hundred years ago I should have tried a silver bullet. Not that I wanted to hurt him or anyone else. It was missing I hated. That's the beast-liest thing in war, the damnable frivolity.

assault signaled the end of the struggle for Verdun, a con-test which had lasted 10 months and cost the French 362,000 men against a German figure of 336,000. The French had held Verdun, the army battered but intact. Falkenhayn's plan had failed, and he was dismissed on 27 August to be replaced by the 'Eastern' team of Hinden-burg and Ludendorff.

All through the first half of 1916 there were French demands for Haig to commit his forces in order to relieve German pressure on Verdun. Although BEF numbers were rising steadily (36 divisions in December 1915, 58 by June 1916), Haig knew that they were insufficiently trained and equipped, and so fought to prevent them being frit-tered away before the great summer offensive. His army was the visible product of an economic and social revo-lution in Britain. Whole new industries were created to meet the unprecedented demand for war materials. Millions of men were removed from civilian life while demands for manpower in industry grew constantly. For the first time, large numbers of women took jobs previous-ly exclusive to men and began to make a major contribu-tion to the wartime economy.

The character of the great Allied offensive of 1916 changed drastically as the Battle of Verdun wore on. Originally conceived as a massive French attack with sub-stantial British backing, it had become apparent by June that the British would have to take the leading role. The original allocation of 40 French divisions to the offensive had progressively fallen to just 12. The location of the offensive decided by General Joffre, however, remained unchanged: the junction of the two armies just north of the River Somme.

The main attack was to be made by the recently formed British Fourth Army under General Sir Henry Rawlinson. Fourteen divisions were deployed for the first assault, supported by five French divisions south of the Somme. The British relied heavily on their enormously expanded artillery arm and lavish ammunition supplies. Rawlinson had 2029 guns and howitzers for his 14-mile frontage. The artillery fired no fewer than 1,732,873 rounds during their eight-day preliminary bombardment. Only 452 guns, however, were heavies (compared with 700 on the French front, which was only half as wide) and some 30 percent of the ammunition supplied by the new industries was to prove defective. Added to this, the strength of the Ger-man positions, with shelters dug deep into the chalk downs of Picardy, was unappreciated by the British.

The Germans had made good use of their 20-month occupation of the Somme region by building an extensive defensive system. In contrast to the Allies, who con-sidered their trenches to be an essentially temporary

ABOVE LEFT: The Allied 'Top Brass' of 1916. From the left: General Joffre, President Poincaré, King George V, General Foch and General Haig. Although Joffre would lose his position as Commander in Chief of the French Army at the end of the year, his compatriot Foch would eventually rise to be Commander in Chief of all the Allied forces on the Western Front – French, British, American and Belgian.

ABOVE: The great attack goes forward – the view toward the German line on 1 July 1916, The First Day of the Battle of the Somme. Particularly distinctive is the white chalk spoil from the forward British trenches, and a German shrapnel shell bursting over the British.

RIGHT: British troops inspect a captured German dugout on the Somme.

BELOW: Major General de Lisle, CO of the 29th Division, addresses one of his units (a battalion of Lancashire Fusiliers) on 29 July 1916.

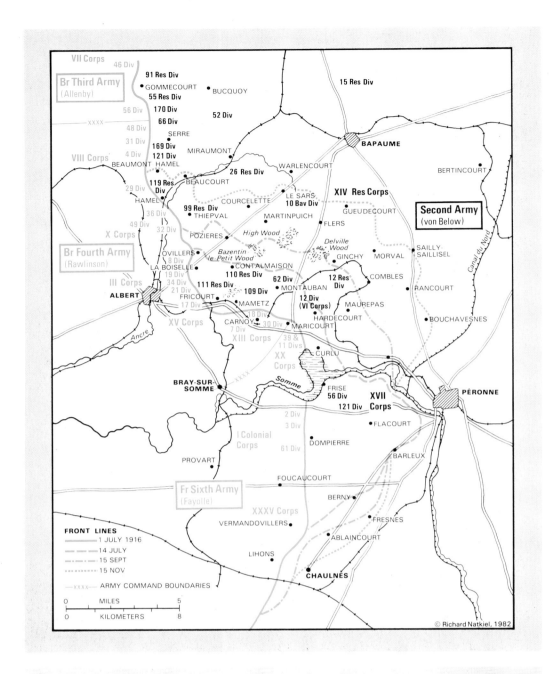

Map labels:
VII Corps — 46 Div
Br Third Army (Allenby)
91 Res Div
GOMMECOURT
55 Res Div • BUCQUOY
15 Res Div
170 Div
56 Div
52 Div
48 Div
66 Div
31 Div
SERRE
4 Div
169 Div MIRAUMONT
121 Div
VIII Corps
BEAUMONT HAMEL
26 Res Div
BAPAUME
WARLENCOURT
BERTINCOURT
119 Res Div
BEAUCOURT
29 Div
HAMEL
COURCELETTE
LE SARS
XIV Res Corps
36 Div
10 Bav Div
THIEPVAL
99 Res Div
MARTINPUICH
GUEUDECOURT
Second Army (von Below)
49 Div
32 Div
POZIERES
High Wood
FLERS
X Corps
Delville Wood
Br Fourth Army (Rawlinson)
OVILLERS
Bazentin le Petit Wood
GINCHY
MORVAL
SAILLY SAILLISEL
8 Div
CONTALMAISON
110 Res Div
III Corps
LA BOISELLE
19 Div
62 Div
12 Res Div
COMBLES
RANCOURT
ALBERT
34 Div
111 Res Div
MONTAUBAN
12 Div (VI Corps)
21 Div
FRICOURT
109 Div
MAUREPAS
BOUCHAVESNES
17 Div
MAMETZ
HARDECOURT
XV Corps
18 Div
CARNOY
30 Div
MARICOURT
7 Div
Ancre
39 & 11 Div
XIII Corps
CURLU
XX Corps
BRAY-SUR-SOMME
Somme
FRISE
56 Div
XVII Corps
PÉRONNE
121 Div
2 Div
FLACOURT
3 Div
I Colonial Corps
DOMPIERRE
61 Div
BARLEUX
PROVART
FOUCAUCOURT
BERNY
Fr Sixth Army (Fayolle)
FRESNES
XXXV Corps
VERMANDOVILLERS
ABLAINCOURT
LIHONS
CHAULNES

FRONT LINES
——— 1 JULY 1916
— — — 14 JULY
— · — 15 SEPT
········· 15 NOV
xxxx ARMY COMMAND BOUNDARIES

MILES 0 — 5
KILOMETERS 0 — 8

© Richard Natkiel, 1982

measure prior to a general advance, the Germans fully exploited the defensive possibilities open to them. Not only were their trench lines built on higher ground overlooking Allied positions, they had also dug deep into the chalk to construct comfortable and, most importantly, shell-proof dugouts. To the largely inexperienced troops of the British Fourth Army, the near constant thunder of the guns persuaded them to accept the pronouncement of their superiors that the capture of the German positions would be a literal 'walk-over.'

The BEF of the summer of 1916 was a unique force comprising three distinct elements. Supplementing the remnants of the old Regular Army were the Territorial divisions, originally a home defense force. Unlike their French namesakes, however, they were quality troops fit for more than just 'line-filling.' Despite this, the majority of the British soldiers on the Somme were Kitchener's volunteers of 1914-15, the enthusiastic but inexperienced troops who made up the New Army. A distinctive feature of the New Army was the way in which local organizations, towns, firms, municipal bodies and other occupational groups formed their own battalions with their own *ésprit de corps*. Assigned nominal unit designations, they were better known by their local nicknames. Battalions such as the 10th East Yorks (Hull Commercials), 15th Lancashire Fusiliers (1st Salford Pals), 16th Highland Light Infantry (Glasgow Boys' Brigade) and 10th Lincolns (Grimsby Chums) were to play a significant role in the coming battle and, along with other New Army units, were largely to be destroyed on the Somme. By contrast, the troops on the other side of No Man's Land were professionals; the German Army was still led by prewar officers and NCOs who provided it with a breadth of experience unknown to the British forces.

Although Haig would have preferred to launch his offensive farther north in Flanders he acquiesced to Joffre's requests for an attack on the Somme where the French and British lines met. Haig, ever optimistic, hoped for a possible breakthrough which, once achieved, could allow the reserves (the Fifth Army under General Sir Hubert Gough) to wheel round northward to roll up the German line. Rawlinson, entrusted with the initial assault, was less optimistic and favored a slower, more methodical advance. Haig believed in giving his army commanders independence of action and, with certain misgivings, deferred for the most part to Rawlinson's wishes. The British plan was simple. Once the artillery had done its work in pulverizing the German trenches and cutting the wire, the heavily laden British infantry would advance across No Man's Land in close-formed lines.

ABOVE LEFT: *The Battle of the Somme.*

LEFT: *The First Day of the Somme – British troops clamber over their own wire.*

RIGHT: *British troops of the 31st Division march up to the trenches at Doullens, 28 June 1916. This platoon is from the 10th East Yorks, better known as the Hull Commercials, one of the four 'Pals' battalions.*

TOP RIGHT: *A British 12-inch gun pounds a German strongpoint.*

ABOVE RIGHT: *Indian cavalry move up to the front line.*

FAR RIGHT: *A wounded Senegalese soldier returns.*

The artillery bombardment increased in intensity during the last 24 hours before zero hour, and for good measure a series of massive land mines were detonated minutes before the signal to attack. Confident that the artillery had done its job, the British infantry went over the top in perfect order at 0730 hours on 1 July – only to be cut down in waves. For as the Allied guns paused, the German defenders – most having survived the bombardment – raced from their dugouts, set up their machine guns and began the massacre of the long lines of khaki-clad infantry moving slowly into view. At the same time the German guns – which had remained largely concealed in anticipation of the assault – began a deadly fire on the British trenches. There, units in the process of forming up, ready to advance, were in a vulnerable position. Some were so badly knocked about they were rendered incapable of further offensive action.

The slaughter was prodigious. The 10th West Yorks lost 710 men in their attack against Fricourt and by the evening the battalion consisted of just one officer and 20 men; the 16th Highland Light Infantry, part of the 32nd Division's assault on Thiepval, lost half its strength in the first 10 minutes. Of those troops who did manage to penetrate the German defenses – the 56th (London) Division to the south of Gommecourt and the 36th (Ulster) Division between the Ancre River and Thiepval – many were forced to withdraw in the face of fierce German counterattacks and, more particularly, because of the failure of adjacent formations to push forward. Only on the right of the British line was progress made. The 18th (Eastern) Division and the 30th Division (alongside the French 39th Division), achieved their initial objectives which included the capture of the village of Montauban. This was the only real British success in a day of complete disaster which saw most British divisions stopped in their tracks or flung back to their start lines. During the evening several German officers, sickened by the slaughter, allowed temporary truces so that some of the badly wounded could be recovered. Other casualties crawled in under cover of night, but many lay undiscovered until after they had died of their wounds. A total of 57,470 British officers and men became casualties on that day, about 20,000 being killed outright. It was the highest daily casualty figure for any army in the history of modern warfare.

The French whose attack supported by plentiful artillery took the Germans by surprise made considerable gains at relatively small cost. The contrast between their flexible infantry tactics and the straight rigid lines of the British advance – offering wonderful targets for artillery and machine guns – has prompted many to blame British

LEFT: *Although making themselves a vulnerable target, a stretcher-bearer team carries a wounded man over the top of a trench in the village of Thiepval. The defenses around Thiepval were among the strongest in the whole sector and the Germans fought desperately to hold the Thiepval Ridge. Despite the fact that it was a first day objective, the position only fell to the British at the end of October.*

RIGHT: *A symbol of British optimism – British cavalry advances toward Hardecourt Wood to support the Flers-Courcelette battle of 15 September in the vain hope of exploiting a breakthrough.*

BELOW: *Men of the 18th Division look over wounded German prisoners walking toward captivity after the Battle of Guillement, 3 September.*

BELOW RIGHT: *British troops receive their dinner rations from field kitchens, Ancre sector, October 1916. Beside its obvious nutritional value, hot food did much to sustain the morale of cold and exhausted men.*

tactics for the heavy loss. The chief reason, however, was the failure of the artillery to overwhelm the defenders. The British had more guns than ever before, but still not enough. They clearly needed larger mountains of ammunition, preferably without defects.

The 1st of July 1916 was a freak event in the war. Never again did the British suffer losses on such a scale and never again during the Battle of the Somme did the French prove so successful. There was no question of discontinuing the offensive – the first day of the Somme was the 132nd day of the Battle of Verdun, and it would have been unthinkable for the British to cease fighting after only one day (even if the Germans had permitted it). The German response was, in any case, extremely vigorous, giving the battle the savage quality it retained to the end. General von Below, commanding their Second Army, told his men on 3 July: 'The important ground lost in certain places will be recaptured . . . the important thing is to hold our present positions at any cost . . . the enemy should have to carve his way over heaps of corpses.' These orders account for the 330 German attacks or counterattacks which punctuated the Allied advances on the Somme.

The British attacks continued. A dawn attack on 14 July showed what the Kitchener Armies were capable of, and indicated considerable improvements in British staff work. Its success surprised both the Germans and the more unimaginative British regular officers. Yet every success turned into trench wafare, with the British slogging on as the counterattacks came in. The devastated villages and strongpoints along the original German line fell remorselessly to the British advance. More and more divisions were fed into the assault, including troops from the Empire (only a battalion of Newfoundlanders from Canada had been present on 1 July, but had suffered 684 casualties, losses second only to the 10th West Yorks). The ruins

of Pozieres fell to a dashing Australian assault on 23 July; the South African Brigade battled for Delville Wood while Canadians and New Zealanders were heavily committed in later attacks.

The 15th of September marked a historic occasion: the first use of tanks in battle – a British innovation. The few Mk I tanks available were no war-winners but their successors were to make a significant contribution in the future. More important was the fact that, for the only time in the war, the Allies managed to strike simultaneous blows: a final offensive by the Russians in the East, the Rumanian entry into the war, an Italian offensive, and attacks by both the British and the French. The Central Powers were badly shaken, but held on.

The final act of the battle was the capture of Beaumont Hamel on 13 November. The battle area was already turning into a sea of mud, and the snows and frosts of the war's worst winter had begun. So the great offensive ended in disappointment and heavy losses for all. British casualties during the 142 days of the Somme amounted to 415,000; the French, even in a secondary role, lost over 200,000; German losses were so great they deliberately disguised them. They probably equaled those of the British and French together.

Taken in conjunction with their losses at Verdun and in repelling the powerful Russian offensives of the year, it was concluded that the old peace-trained German Army had now disappeared. The Somme, Germany later admitted, was 'the muddy grave of the German field army.' The British, on the other hand, had now attained professional status and, with only two short intermissions, it would be the BEF which henceforth engaged the main body of the German Army in battle until it was defeated.

LEFT: Rockets and other incendiary flares rise into the early morning sky prior to the assault on Thiepval, 15 September 1916. When troops in a frontline trench felt threatened, they would send up variously colored 'SOS' rockets to alert their own artillery to lay down a defensive barrage against the enemy.

RIGHT: The winter of 1916-17 was considered to be the worst in living memory and trench warfare made conditions unbearable at times. These British troops prepare for the hopeless task of clearing mud from this trench near Trones Wood, November 1916.

BELOW LEFT: A general view of Beaumont Hamel at the end of the Battle of the Somme, November 1916. The heap of bricks in the center is the remains of the village church.

BELOW: One of the human casualties of the Somme. Totaling well over one million casualties, the Somme has been reckoned to be the bloodiest battle in history.

CHAPTER SIX

STRUGGLE FOR THE HIGH SEAS

If Germany was considered the leading military power in 1914, the position of major naval power was undisputably held by Britain. No serious challenge to the Royal Navy's supremacy had been made from the fall of Napoleon in 1815 until the early years of the twentieth century, when a new threat was posed by the emergence of a powerful and growing Imperial German Navy. Under the energetic leadership of Admiral Alfred von Tirpitz the German *Kriegsmarine* had become a potent force – inferior in size to the Royal Navy but sufficient to alarm the British into improving and increasing the size of their own fleet.

In 1906 Admiral Sir John Fisher brought about a true revolution in warship design with the launch of HMS *Dreadnought*, the first big-gun, turbine-driven battleship which rendered all existing battleships (including Britain's huge pre-dreadnought fleet) obsolete. Henceforward, surface navies would be measured by their dreadnought strength: in 1914 Britain had 20 in commission and 12 being built, while Germany had 16 and four being built. To the Admiralty, with its worldwide responsibilities, this margin seemed none too large.

These huge ships, with their attendant swarms of cruisers and destroyers, their long-range guns and ever more destructive shells, their massive armor, their optical equipment for range-finding, their speed and their radio communications, brought about a re-evaluation of the naval profession. The range and variety of change that swept through the naval world was bewildering and, indeed, the swiftness of the transformation led to a genuine technological revolution. For example, at the turn of the century the effective range of the main armament of a battleship was around 4000 yards; by 1914 this had increased to distances of up to 20,000 yards. Paradoxically, as the battleship increased its striking power, the development of the torpedo made it vulnerable to submarines and small surface vessels. A torpedo boat was, in theory, capable of sinking a 20,000-ton battleship. To counter this danger the battleship acquired a defensive

PREVIOUS PAGES: HMS Canopus *in the Gallipoli campaign.*

ABOVE, FAR LEFT: Grand Admiral Alfred von Tirpitz, father of the German Navy.

ABOVE LEFT: Admiral Sir John Fisher played a key role in modernizing the Royal Navy.

ABOVE: Wilhelm II dressed up to play the 'Supreme War Lord' of the oceans.

LEFT: The root cause of Anglo-German antagonism, a German dreadnought.

BELOW: A German warship heads out to sea.

RIGHT AND BELOW RIGHT: Two scenes from the Battle of Coronel depicting the Scharnhorst *and* Gneisenau.

screen of destroyers and other similar craft. The destroyer emerged as a most potent and flexible warship, capable of steaming at a speed of 40 knots and armed with both guns and torpedoes, the latter capable of hitting a target up to five miles away.

Beside these dramatic improvements in the warship's fighting abilities, the development of wireless telegraphy and naval aviation took naval strategy and tactics into a new dimension. Yet neither the German nor the British navies had had the chance to deploy their fearsome new weapons in earnest. The naval planners' theories were, in the last resort, just detailed guesswork and, not surprisingly, the admirals erred on the side of caution.

The Royal Navy acted as the nation's shield, protecting the United Kingdom from assault and invasion, while safeguarding Britain's far-flung and extensive commercial interests around the globe. No other country relied so heavily on maritime trade and an effective Royal Navy was, quite simply, vital to British survival. Command of the high seas had the corollary of denying it to the enemy, and the Germans had few illusions regarding the survival of their overseas trade and empire once Britain joined the war. As long as the Royal Navy retained its pre-eminent position it could extend its role to the direct help of its allies and the direct hindrance of Germany and her allies. If this position were lost, however, and Germany's Navy gained control, Britain would be faced with disaster. Such massive responsibility weighed heavily on the Commander in Chief of Britain's Grand Fleet, Admiral Sir John Jellicoe, and Winston Churchill was hardly exaggerating when he said of Jellicoe: 'He is the only man on either side who could lose the war in an afternoon.'

Consequently the purpose of the Imperial German Navy, and the High Seas Fleet concentrated in the North Sea in particular, was to inflict – or threaten to inflict – such damage on the Royal Navy that British supremacy at sea would be irretrievably lost. The German public expected dramatic action, as did the British public who confidently awaited another Trafalgar or, at the very least, the imprisonment of the Germans in their harbors as the French had been by the close-blockading squadrons of Nelson's day. None of these things happened. They were ruled out by the new technology. Close blockade was made impossible by the dual underwater threat of mines-and torpedo-firing submarines. However, the Germans were to discover to their cost that distant blockade (the Grand Fleet's bases at Scapa Flow in the Orkneys and Rosyth in the Firth of Forth were around 600 miles from German naval harbors) could be as effective as the traditional method. It was one of the war's outstanding innovations that, together with the power to communicate across great distances, wireless telegraphy also conferred the power to overhear the enemy. British listening stations made it virtually impossible for the German Navy to make a move without the decoding section – situated in the mysteriously named 'Room 40' – of British naval intelligence being aware of it. The capture of the German naval codes early in the war conferred a priceless advantage; if the British Admiralty was slow to exploit it fully, the Germans were slower still to grasp what had occurred.

At the outbreak of war in August 1914 the Royal Navy was faced with a daunting array of tasks. That it was able to fulfill them all was one of the great achievements of the war. In the first instance the Royal Navy was called upon to sweep the world's oceans of German ships, both to protect Britain's vital maritime trade and to deny Germany any global advantage. In addition, the Navy transported and protected millions of men from Britain and the Empire as they were shipped around the globe to the various theaters of war. Most important of all, the Navy established, by stages, a supply blockade against the Central Powers. Once the generals had failed to force a military decision by the end of 1914, the 'total war' dimension expanded accordingly and the Royal Navy's patient and largely successful blockade was an important factor in the collapse of Germany in 1918.

The spectacle now unfolded of the two main fleets, numbering over 250 vessels, lying for the most part idly at anchor, while the crises of the naval war developed elsewhere. German shipping (naval and mercantile) was swept from the seas by British supremacy from the outset, providing the British mercantile marine with the freedom of the seas. This action allowed the German 'U' (*Untersee*)-boats an abundance of targets, whereas the Royal Navy's submarines had to search perilous waters to find them. However, it was the Royal Navy who first drew blood in the underwater war. The first action between surface and submarine craft was the ramming and sinking of U-15 by HMS *Birmingham* on 9 August 1914. The first sinking of a warship by a submarine was the destruction of HMS *Pathfinder* by U-21 on 3 September. The first sinking by a British submarine was on 13 September: the cruiser *Hela* by E-9. The first sinking of a submarine by another submarine was E-3 by U-27 on 18 October. A new and deadly style of war was then heralded by the first sinking of a merchant ship by a submarine: the British steamer *Glitra* by U-17 on 20 October. The first merchantman to be sunk without warning was the French *Admiral Ganteaume* by U-24 on 26 October. A new chapter of naval history was being written; the declaration of a submarine blockade of British waters came in February 1915.

The first U-boat campaign lasted just over a year. Its most spectacular feat was the sinking of the Cunard liner *Lusitania* on 7 May 1915 without warning; 1198 lives were lost, of whom 159 were Americans. This marked a key stage in the alienation of neutral opinion which culminated just under two years later in America's declaration of war against Germany. There was little else to show for the first U-boat campaign; since Germany possessed only 21 U-boats in the North Sea at the start (of which only three or four could be maintained simultaneously on patrol), this was hardly surprising. Fortunately for the Allies, the German Navy had made a cardinal error in

Naval Gunnery

In the last quarter of the nineteenth century, the number of large guns carried in capital ships decreased but their range, accuracy and destructive power increased enormously. The introduction of the dreadnought-type battleship speeded this process up, so that a 1914 British battleship might typically mount 10 12-inch guns (main armament) and 16 4-inch guns (secondary). During the war bigger-gunned ships began to appear, the Germans introducing the Baden class (eight 15-inch guns) and the British the Queen Elizabeth class (eight 15-inch guns) – probably the finest battleship class to see action during World War I. These huge guns were capable of firing shells weighing nearly a ton to a distance of 15,000 yards.

These dramatic improvements in gun technology brought their own problems, particularly that of accuracy. To hit a moving enemy vessel steaming at up to 20 knots, when your own ship was moving at a similar speed on a different bearing at a distance of over 10,000 yards in less than perfect visibility, would have been almost impossible had it not been for developments in fire-control systems and optical rangefinders. British gunnery standards declined during the nineteenth century until the arrival of two influential gunnery officers, Admiral Sir John Fisher and Captain Percy Scott, who forced the Royal Navy to incorporate the latest methods and improve upon them.

All the main guns came under the centralized control of the ship's fire-direc-tor who would receive information on the intended target's course and speed. This was then computed against the firing vessel's course and speed, while other variables – wind speed and direction, the time it would take the shells to hit their target – were also taken into account. The development of the Dreyer Fire Control Table meant that this early computer could, in a matter of seconds, assess the information and provide a series of elevation and training settings for the main armament. Once these had been made ready, the fire-control officer would fire a simultaneous salvo. Constant gunnery practice should ensure that the salvo of shots fell in a tight group, so that the fall of shot could be spotted by the officer in the high control top and corrections made – up or down, left or right – until the salvo pattern fell on the target.

While the British pioneered the fire-control systems, the German Navy possessed superior long-range stereoscopic rangefinders. These could ascertain the correct range faster than the British system of ranging salvoes, but depended on the optical skills of highly trained rangefinders and were subject to the vagaries of visibility. Both the German and British Navies placed great emphasis on improving their gunnery in the years leading up to the war, although on balance it would seem that the Germans had the edge in accuracy. At Jutland, the German battlecruiser squadron was certainly much more proficient than that of the Royal Navy.

TOP LEFT: HMS Dreadnought, *the ship that transformed naval warfare at a stroke.*

CENTER LEFT: Early victim of a sea mine, HMS Audacious *goes down off the north coast of Ireland, 27 October 1914. Displacing 23,370 tonnes the* Audacious *was one of the Royal Navy's latest battleships, and her loss encouraged a healthy respect for the naval mine.*

LEFT: A German U-boat fires its deck gun, the usual weapon employed against 'soft' targets like merchantmen. Torpedoes were to be saved for warships or merchant ships under escort.

RIGHT: A photograph taken from a German U-boat depicting the last minutes of the American tanker SS Illinois, *sunk by the submarine in the English Channel. The death of American nationals in incidents such as this turned US public opinion against Germany.*

LEFT: *A night action at sea.*

RIGHT: *A German submarine closes in to inspect a suspect merchantman.*

BELOW LEFT: *Plumes of water are thrown up by near-misses in a naval battle.*

BELOW: *A line of battle opens fire in a surface engagement.*

attempting to emulate the style and organization of its main rival, the Royal Navy, instead of pursuing the more effective policy of building a navy which could inflict the most harm on Britain. Accordingly, the *Kriegsmarine* poured its resources into building massive and expensive capital ships; the more cost-effective U-boat arm was correspondingly neglected. Nevertheless, the sinking of 1,328,985 gross tonnes of Allied shipping during the year was a significant pointer to the future.

Surface warfare, meanwhile, continued on more familiar lines. It was a blow to British naval prestige when the German ships *Goeben* and *Breslau* escaped unharmed from the Mediterranean to Constantinopole, precipitating Turkish entry into the war. This disappointment for the British public was balanced by the news of a successful Royal Navy action off the Heligoland Bight on 28 August 1914. Supported by the battlecruisers of Admiral Sir David Beatty, Commodore Reginald Tyrwhitt's Harwich Flotilla trapped a force of German light cruisers in the chain of islands off the German coast. In the ensuing engagement three German light cruisers and a destroyer were sunk (with a loss of over 1000 men) while the British lost only 35 men and no ships. The victory seemed impressive but it remained a minor action and one which concealed alarming errors of signaling and command on the British side. These failings were glossed over in the subsequent victory celebrations, only to reappear more damagingly later on in the sea war.

The Germans scored their own 'publicity' victory when their raiding squadrons were able to reach and bombard towns on the east coast of England and escape with impunity. A populace totally unschooled in the character of modern naval war was much dismayed by this. The knowledge that German warships had stood off the east coast towns of Scarborough and Hartlepool, shelling the defenseless civilian population, suggested to the public that there were serious holes in Britannia's shield. In Scarborough 17 people were killed and 80 wounded, while the figures for Hartlepool were 113 dead and at least 300 wounded. Supported by photographs in the popular press of devastated buildings, these casualty lists led to public

TOP: A dramatic shot of the German armored cruiser Blücher *turning turtle following her pounding by British battlecruisers at the Battle of Dogger Bank, 24 January 1915.*

ABOVE: Damage inflicted upon houses in Hartlepool after shelling by German warships, 16 December 1914.

LEFT: The loss of the British battlecruiser Queen Mary *at the Battle of Jutland, 31 May 1916.*

BELOW: Commander of the German East Asiatic Squadron, Vice-Admiral Graf von Spee.

ABOVE: *Captain Karl von Müller, the chivalrous commander of the* Emden.

RIGHT: *The remains of the* Emden, *November 1914.*

BELOW RIGHT: *The Emden before the war.*

BOTTOM RIGHT: *A scene from the Dogger Bank engagement.*

uproar, an impotent waving of fists which would be repeated in 1917 following the Gotha bombing raids on London. Even in this relatively small way, modern war had directly touched the public consciousness.

Improved radio surveillance of German movements was making all such activities more hazardous. Both the Hartlepool and Scarborough raids in December 1914 and the Dogger Bank action in January 1915 came close to causing disaster for the Germans. The Dogger Bank battle of 24 January 1915 was the most important engagement of North Sea cat-and-mouse strategy before Jutland. The German battlecruiser squadron intended to destroy British scouting ships and fishing vessels operating over the Dogger Bank. Forewarned by naval intelligence, however, a powerful counterforce of British battle-cruisers, again under the command of Beatty, steamed southward to intercept.

On sighting the British ships bearing down on them, the Germans promptly turned for home and a long-range running battle ensued between the two battlecruiser squadrons. Again, a significant British victory was thwarted by poor communication. The German battle-cruisers – including the severely damaged *Seydlitz* – managed to escape, largely because the leading British ships had concentrated their fire on the ageing armored cruiser *Blücher*, which was admittedly sunk in spectacu-lar fashion. While the British again failed to profit from their errors, the Germans realized the vulnerability of modern warships to flash-fires and immediately intro-duced anti-flash safeguards. The British learned the same lesson only after several of their ships were lost at the Battle of Jutland due to unprotected magazines.

Both encounters with superior British forces instilled in the Germans a great respect for British naval intelligence, though they never realized where they were going wrong. Over a year would pass before the German battle squad-rons ventured into the North Sea again, a victory for wire-less telegraphy, interception and cryptanalysis. Such secret matters were known to few; what was obvious to the public was the progress of surface warfare where it could be observed by neutrals and newspaper reporters. The raiding activities of German light cruisers in distant waters – in particular the *Emden* under her skillful and chivalrous Captain Karl von Müller in the Indian Ocean – attracted much attention. One by one, however, the cruisers were eliminated, radio or radio interception play-ing a major role in their destruction.

The most powerful German cruiser force was Vice-Admiral Maximilian von Spee's East Asiatic Squadron in

ABOVE: The German commerce raider Seeadler *which operated with great success off the Norwegian coast disguised as an innocent cargo ship.*

ABOVE RIGHT: HMS Inflexible *(background) picks up survivors from the* Gneisenau, *sunk off the Falkland Islands, 8 December 1914.*

BELOW: Rear Admiral Sir Christopher Cradock, killed at Cape Coronel.

BOTTOM: Admiral Sir John Jellicoe, commander of the British Grand Fleet.

the Pacific. This consisted of the two heavy cruisers, *Scharnhorst* and *Gneisenau*, displacing 11,600 tons and each with eight 21cm and six 15cm guns, plus three light cruisers of the *Emden* type. Against Spee was arrayed an Australian squadron in the South Seas which included the fast, modern battlecruiser *Australia* (18,800 tons) with eight 12-inch guns, itself capable of destroying the whole German squadron alone. When Japan entered the war on 23 August she added to the Allied strength two modern battlecruisers capable of 27 knots and four smaller ones. Faced with this, Spee had little choice: he set course across the Pacific and on 1 November his crack heavy cruisers sank the two elderly British cruisers *Good Hope* and *Monmouth* under Rear Admiral Sir Christopher Cradock at Cape Coronel off the coast of South America.

The British response was swift and devastating. The new First Sea Lord, Admiral Fisher, dispatched two battlecruisers of his own design, *Invincible* and *Inflexible* (armed like *Australia* with 12-inch guns), under Vice-Admiral Sir Doveton Sturdee to the Falkland Islands. The plan was to bar Spee's passage into the Atlantic, and on 8 December the rival forces met. After a long-running fight all the German vessels, except one light cruiser, were sunk. Spee, along with both his sons, died in the action, as did 2000 German sailors. To the British public, a Nelsonian retribution had been inflicted upon an impertinent enemy; the length of time it had taken their great ships to sink the far weaker opponents was of no concern. Few were disposed to question the viability of Fisher's battlecruisers as naval units and nearly 18 months would elapse before the answer became apparent.

In January 1916 Admiral Reinhard von Scheer replaced the overly cautious Admiral von Pohl as Commander in Chief of the Imperial German Navy. An energetic and forceful personality, Scheer was bound to try and bring the Royal Navy to battle in a major fleet action on, hopefully, Germany's terms. Scheer's enterprizing new policy brought about the one great naval battle of World War I on 31 May 1916. Known by the British as the Battle of Jutland (and by the Germans as the Battle of Skagerrak), this action saw the involvement of 259 warships.

German strategy remained basically the same: an

attempt to maneuver the British Grand Fleet into battle with only part of its strength facing the entire German High Seas Fleet. The British response was also familiar: radio surveillance enabled the Grand Fleet to put to sea before the Germans had even left harbor. Admiral Jellicoe took his Grand Fleet from Scapa Flow on an intercepting course with Admiral Beatty's battlecruiser squadrons and four new fast battleships, based at Rosyth, scouting ahead. Cruisers from Beatty's squadron made contact off Jutland with German scouting vessels and soon the British battlecruisers sighted Vice-Admiral Franz von Hipper's battlecruiser squadron screening the advance of the main German fleet. Battle was joined between these scouting groups in the afternoon. German gunnery and armor protection proved superior to that of the British and in this preliminary engagement two of Beatty's battlecruisers – *Indefatigable* and *Queen Mary* – were blown up. Despite these setbacks, Beatty, who had caught sight of the German battleships approaching from the south, continued to maneuver so as to draw the Germans on to the main British force.

Beatty, however, was not keeping Jellicoe informed of the enemy's position and course. Jellicoe's problem lay in choosing the best possible moment for deploying his battlefleet of 24 dreadnoughts which were moving in six parallel columns, a formation suitable for cruising in search of the enemy but less appropriate for fighting a battle. In battle, line ahead gave all ships a chance to use their guns, and Jellicoe had to deploy into line ahead before the enemy was in range but not before he knew the enemy's position and bearing. At 1815 hours the German battlecruisers encountered the three battlecruisers which had served to screen Jellicoe. Again German gunnery proved devastatingly successful and a third British battlecruiser, *Invincible*, was blown apart. However, Jellicoe was now able to calculate the likely position of the main German forces. He started his masterly deployment into line ahead and 20 minutes later the unsuspecting Scheer, with his battleships in line ahead, was confronted by the British battlefleet passing ahead of him at right angles. With all the British battleships able to concentrate their gunfire on his leading ships, Scheer was in a perilous

TOP: *A scene from the battlecruiser action at the Battle of Jutland.*

ABOVE CENTER: *Vice-Admiral Hipper, the German battlecruiser commander at Jutland.*

ABOVE: *Admiral Scheer, Commander in Chief of the High Seas Fleet.*

RIGHT: *The fleets close on each other as Jutland develops into a full-scale battleship action.*

The Battle of Jutland

Jutland was the one major naval battle of the war, and was the last great clash of massed 'battle' ships in naval history. For the men involved it was a confusing affair and this account from the officer of the fore-turret of HMS *Indomitable* reflects his own special viewpoint of the war's major naval battle:

We were now (6.20pm) heavily engaged with the enemy battle-cruisers and with, I think, the head of his battle line, the range being 8200 yards, bearing 90 Green. Suddenly my left gun ceased firing. The thin metal bulkhead which had been built round the sighting position to render it, as far as possible, soundproof prevented me from seeing what was wrong, and for a few moments I could get no reply to my enquiries from the loading officer. This was exasperating and I began to fear that the turret had been hit, although I had felt no concussion, when the welcome report came that it was only a cordite charge that had jammed and broken up.

At 6.35pm we altered course slightly to port, reverting to controlled fire at a range of 10,700 yards. Then upon the starboard bow I saw the two ends of a ship standing perpendicularly above water, the ship appearing to have broken in halves amidships, each half resting on the bottom. My gunlayer took her for a Hun and the crew cheered, but I could read the name *Invincible* on the stern and so knew better. Four or five survivors were clinging to floating wreckage; I have never seen anything more splendid than these few cheering us as we raced by them.

We could now see the battle fleet coming up astern in three columns, and at 7.12pm they reopened fire. The spectacle was truly magnificent,

tongues of flame seeming to leap from end to end of the line, but owing to the dusk and smoke we could not see what practice they were making. At 7.20pm we reopened fire at the enemy battle-cruisers at a range of 14,000 yards, our squadron apparently making splendid practice. Time after time, a dull orange glow would appear on board one or other of their ships, a glow which increased and brightened then slowly dulled; yet, in spite of these hits, the enemy's volume of fire did not seem appreciably to diminish. One big ship turned out of her line to starboard, her after-part enveloped in flame, and began slowly to drop astern.

At 8.20pm, unexpectedly, the enemy battlecruisers were again sighted closing toward us, and a few seconds later they opened fire. Most of my turret's crew had come up on top for a breath of fresh air and to hunt for splinters as souvenirs, so they tumbled back to their stations in a hurry, and by 8.26pm we were hard at it again at a range of 8800 yards. The German firing was fairly good and we were straddled several times. Many of our squadron's salvoes were hits, and large fires were observed on board several of their ships, and their speed seemed to decrease. At 8.42pm they had had enough and drew off so we ceased firing, although other ships in the squadron continued for a little time longer.

Should it be my good fortune to be engaged in another action, I shall take care that only one gramophone is taken into the turret. In my turret we had two, one in the gun-house and one in the working chamber, and during every lull in the action these two were started playing simultaneously, each with a different record. The result was one of the real horrors of the war.

situation. As his ships began to suffer serious damage from the accurate fire of the British battleships, Scheer ordered them to do a 180-degree 'battleturn,' a difficult maneuver to perform. Half an hour later Scheer again found his 'T' completely crossed by the Grand Fleet. Once more there was a brief exchange of fire while the Germans withdrew under cover of a smokescreen. This time, German destroyers launched a torpedo attack on the British. Jellicoe turned away and lost contact with the Germans. He was later criticized for this move but Churchill was probably right when he later emphasized the enormous responsibility carried by Jellicoe.

During the night Jellicoe tried to interpose his ships between the fleeing Germans and their bases. Confusion within the Admiralty meant vital intercepted German radio messages failed to get through, while negligent British commanders failed to report their ships' actions with the enemy during the night. Consequently the Germans were able to slip back to their ports. The long-awaited encounter between the two fleets had ended unsatisfactorily for the British. They had lost three battle-cruisers and three armored cruisers against a German loss of one battlecruiser, one old battleship and three armored cruisers. Britain's casualty total of 6107 was slightly less than double that of the Germans (3058 men). Once again poor British signaling had deprived the Royal Navy of a great victory. Added to this were failures in British battlecruiser gunnery compounded by poor quality armor-piercing shells, and finally and most significantly, insufficient protection from flash-fire explosions.

German propaganda was quick to capitalize on the scale of Royal Navy losses at Jutland but, while Scheer had conducted the battle with considerable coolness and his ships had fought well, the Germans had fled the scene of the battle, leaving the British in command of the North Sea. A tactical draw, Jutland was a strategic victory for Britain: the German High Seas Fleet played no further significant part in the war until November 1918 when its demoralized crews broke out into open mutiny. Thus the *Kriegsmarine* had been unable to break the Royal Navy's blockade of the Central Powers, which from 1916 onward was to tighten its stranglehold. Among the many newspaper reports on the consequences of Jutland, one American journalist summed it up most aptly: 'The German fleet has assaulted its jailor, but it is still in jail.'

ABOVE LEFT: *The severely damaged German battlecruiser Seydlitz in harbor after her battering at Jutland.*

ABOVE: *A depiction of the daring exploit undertaken by the commander of the German Zeppelin L23 in capturing the Norwegian sailing ship Royal.*

LEFT: *German warships make steam as they head out to sea in the hope of cutting off the British battlecruisers at Jutland, 31 May 1916.*

RIGHT: *A German warship prepares to leave harbor as smoke billows from her funnels.*

In the Mediterranean the Allies maintained overall naval supremacy and surface actions were few, although ships of the Austro-Hungarian Navy made occasional sorties into the Adriatic Sea. In order to prevent Austrian warships breaking out into the Mediterranean proper, the Allies constructed a barrage of small vessels across the Straits of Otranto at the southern end of the Adriatic. Although the barrage was less than successful, Austrian warships presented little threat to the Anglo-French fleets. The real danger lay in German U-boat action against Allied merchant shipping. It was in the Mediterranean that the famous (or infamous) U-35 carried out most of her sinkings: a total of 224 ships, making her the most successful submarine of all time.

In the Black Sea there were clashes between the Turkish and Russian Navies, but these had no influence on the course of the war. The largest area of maritime activity in the Mediterranean was the naval support provided during the Dardanelles campaign. Firstly, in the unsuccessful attempt to force the Dardanelles Straits by naval action alone and, secondly, in the transportation of ground forces in the equally unsuccessful land battle for the Gallipoli Peninsula.

As the summer of 1916 wore on, with the Eastern Front once more aflame and the Battle of the Somme reaching a climax, Germany's position became desperate. The demand for 'unrestricted' U-boat warfare became more urgent than ever and was now backed by the Army High Command. By October, the U-boats had effectively settled the matter. A sharp rise in the number of attacks without warning brought a significant rise in the amount of shipping sunk. From October 1916 to October 1917 the monthly world total never fell below 300,000 tonnes. On 1 February 1917, this state of affairs received formal recognition. The 'unrestricted' campaign was declared, and at once produced alarming results for the Allies: 584,671 tonnes of shipping were sunk that month, 603,369 in March and a record figure of 894,147 tonnes in April.

The German High Command was to pay a heavy price for its advocacy of unrestricted submarine warfare. American public opinion was becoming more anti-German as the numbers of American civilians lost at sea through U-boat action increased. By early 1917 American industry had become a major supplier for the Allies, and in so doing had become a close economic partner. The U-boat campaign gave the US government the rationale to extend the trans-Atlantic partnership still further, so that on the 6 April 1917 America declared war on Germany. From then on, unless Germany could win a quick and resounding military victory on the Western Front, the balance of forces would move in favor of the Allies.

At the same time the U-boat success caused grave concern for the governments of the Western Allies and there seemed a very real possibility that the Allies might lose the war, with the cutting-off of overseas supplies on which they (Britain above all) depended. The remainder of the war at sea was, in fact, the war against the U-boats. This was decided partly by method – the revival of the convoy system on which British trade had always depended in war – and partly by technology. Convoys made it increasingly difficult for U-boats to find and attack targets. Technology (depth charges, improved mines, hydrophones, increasing use of aircraft and always the contribution of radio-based intelligence) steadily overcame the U-boat advantages of invisibility and surprise. In April 1918, for the first time, Allied shipping production exceeded losses, marking the defeat of the U-boats. By the end of the war, no fewer than 178 U-boats had been lost, 140 by enemy action. Yet their crews' morale remained high, and as the German Navy collapsed in mutiny and revolution in 1918, only the U-boat crews continued to do their duty, despite casualties amounting to about 30 percent of all who served in the submarine arm.

TOP: A group of escort vessels guard American troopships on their way to Europe. Millions of men crossed the Atlantic in complete safety during 1917-18, largely because of the convoy system.

ABOVE: The Royal Naval Air Service was quick to experiment with a variety of new developments which included a Sopwith Pup making the first successful landing at sea on the aircraft carrier HMS Furious in 1917.

ABOVE RIGHT: German sailors pay out a cable during a mine-laying patrol in enemy waters.

RIGHT: A somewhat fanciful recreation of a sea engagement during World War I.

WAR POSTERS

Despite the absence of radio and television the world of 1914 was one in which the techniques of mass communication had become commonplace. Newspapers were very important but for projecting a simple visual image the poster was supreme. Message and presentation varied to suit particular requirements and the posters here represent a typical cross-section: pleas for money and manpower; celebrations of military prowess; satirical views of the enemy; admonishment not to waste raw materials and simple adverts for war industries.

Food *is*
Ammunition-
Don't waste it.
UNITED STATES FOOD ADMINISTRATION

HILFT UNS IM KAMPFE UM DEN FRIEDEN!

ZEICHNET
KRIEGSANLEIHE.

CACCIALI VIA!
SOTTOSCRIVETE AL PRESTITO

TURN YOUR SILVER INTO BULLETS
AT THE POST OFFICE

CHAPTER SEVEN

A YEAR OF DISAPPOINTMENT

The cost of the great Battles of Verdun and the Somme profoundly shocked the governments of France and Britain. The scale of the military effort and the loss of so many men were without historical precedent and yet, as 1916 drew to a close, the net result was deadlock once again. Demands for change were in the air. In France, Joffre was replaced as Commander in Chief (kicked upstairs to become a Marshal of France) by General Robert Nivelle, an artillery officer who had established a reputation for efficient and successful operations during the French counterattacks at Verdun. In Britain, the Prime Minister, Herbert Asquith, was succeeded by David Lloyd George on 7 December. Always mistrustful of the military, Lloyd George sought to reverse the 'Western' strategy of the Chief of the Imperial General Staff, Sir William Robertson, and Sir Douglas Haig (newly promoted Field Marshal), by advocating an all-out attempt to crush Austria.

Nivelle thought differently: he planned a major French offensive in Champagne, supported by a British attack around Arras. Charming and articulate, Nivelle gained the confidence of the Allied politicians, and his ability to speak good English made a favorable impression on Lloyd George who, despite his fervent 'Eastern' stance, accepted Nivelle's plan for an offensive in the West. In striking contrast to the aloof and attritional-minded Joffre, Nivelle promised the politicans outright victory – quickly and cheaply. War weary, they grasped at Nivelle's almost magical promises and expectations rose accordingly.

Nivelle claimed the battle could be won in 48 hours by an attack of some 1,200,000 men against the German line along the *Chemin des Dames* which overlooked the River Aisne. With over 5000 guns at his disposal Nivelle guaranteed that the German defenses would be pulverized into submission. However, matters were somewhat complicated when the German High Command set in motion a strategic withdrawal along a wide sector of the Western Front on 14 March, falling back to carefully prepared positions some 15 to 20 miles to the rear of the existing line.

The new line became known as the *Siegfried Stellung* to the Germans and the Hindenburg Line to the Allies. Intended primarily as a means of rationalizing the German defenses, the withdrawal shortened the trench lines by 25 miles, allowing some 10 divisions to be withdrawn from frontline duties. The German decision was no doubt influenced by their knowledge of the intended French offensive (French security was virtually non-existent), for the withdrawal seriously dislocated Nivelle's plan. Yet he stubbornly refused to make any operational changes in the face of growing misgivings from both his own army commanders and the British.

The British diversionary attack around Arras opened the 1917 Allied offensive. The Canadian Corps was

PREVIOUS PAGES: The Battle of Vimy Ridge, April 1917.

RIGHT: The magician who failed, General Robert Nivelle.

BELOW: A British 9.45-inch heavy trench mortar is made ready in a captured trench at Gommecourt.

BOTTOM: Canadian troops consolidate their new-won positions on Vimy Ridge, April 1917.

ABOVE: David Lloyd George, Britain's controversial war premier, was constantly at odds with his Western Front generals.

RIGHT: British cavalry ride through Arras to support the advance on Vimy Ridge, April 1917.

BELOW: A column of German prisoners is led away to captivity after the Canadian victory.

ordered to take Vimy Ridge (considered virtually impregnable) in order to safeguard the left flank of the main advance either side of Arras which was entrusted to General Sir Edmund Allenby's Third Army. The German position was well defended but the British had planned the offensive with some care, profiting from the lessons of the Somme battle the previous year.

Artillery support was greatly increased to nearly 3000 guns, a substantial proportion of which were 'heavies' – essential for destroying well-constructed strongpoints. Fire-control tactics had improved, as had the quality of the shells: the number of 'duds' had been greatly reduced and the new '106' fuze made its debut. Constructed to detonate on grazing the ground, the '106' shell had an increased anti-personnel range, was capable of cutting wire more effectively and did less damage to the ground than conventional shells. New gas projectors were in place along the British lines, forcing the Germans into wearing movement-inhibiting gas masks when the attack finally came.

On the German side the new system of flexible defense – instituted by Ludendorff as an antidote to the costly stalemate of the Somme battles – was not fully understood. The British, on the other hand, had thoroughly trained their troops in appropriate opening attack maneuvers. On 9 April (Easter Sunday) the British troops went 'over the top' and made good progress; their methodical preparations had paid off. The four divisions of the Canadian Corps struggled up Vimy Ridge – a honeycomb of defenses which had frustrated previous French attacks with great bloodshed – and after a bitter fight which cost them nearly 10,000 men they won control of the position. Further south the British were similarly successful and a few units advanced to a depth of over three miles on the first day.

Despite their shock the German commanders coolly prevented any Allied breakthrough with their usual adroit handling of reserves and the British advance lost momentum. The original British plan had been to limit the battle once serious resistance was encountered but Haig prolonged the offensive to 23 May in order to provide aid to the French, who had suffered disastrously as their own (Nivelle) offensive collapsed in ruins. From 9 April to 3 May British casualties rose to an official figure of 84,000. In the next, unproductive phase of the battle which carried on to 23 May, the figure grew further to a total of 158,660 killed or wounded.

The Nivelle offensive began on 16 April. The German defense-in-depth defeated Nivelle's artillery gambit and the French infantry paid the price. By the afternoon of the first day the offensive had slowed. However, the French pressed on for a further 10 days, securing limited objectives and capturing over 28,000 Germans in the process. The net result of the offensive was 187,000 French casualties compared with an estimated German minimum of 163,000. A further casualty was Nivelle himself dismissed in favor of General Henri Pétain, the popular 'Savior of Verdun' in 1916.

Compared to 1915 and 1916 the French casualty lists were not high but the French Army had received a near-fatal blow. Nivelle's promises had raised the Army's expectations to a dangerously high level, only to be brutally dashed when his attack failed to penetrate the German line by more than four miles. There was widespread demoralization and mutiny was in the air. On 3 May, some infantry division troops refused to go back into the trenches. By the end of June, units in over 50 divisions had refused to obey orders. Extreme left-wingers were quick to exploit the revolutionary possibilities of the mutiny and there was talk of marching on Paris to overthrow the government. For the vast majority of the troops, however, the mutiny had few political overtones; they regarded their action more as a refusal to be sacrificed on the battlefield at the behest of incompetent generals and callous

ABOVE: *Men of the 12th King's Liverpool Regiment pose by some of the trophies captured by them during the Battle of Arras, 10 April 1917. Behind the group is a mobile German pillbox.*

ABOVE RIGHT: *French prisoners (or deserters) fall back on enemy lines from a village just captured by the Germans.*

RIGHT: *A troop of armored cars is caught up in the streets of Arras, April 1917. These vehicles were built on a basic Rolls Royce chassis and featured a turret-mounted Vickers machine gun. The terrain encountered on the Western Front severely limited the possibilities for operations using armored cars and they were more commonly used in the Middle East.*

politicians. Many agreed to go into the trenches but would not accept orders to attack.

To those in authority the situation seemed desperate indeed but, with Pétain as Commander in Chief, order was slowly restored. Ringleaders were shot (55 official executions; there is no record of unofficial cases) but Pétain remedied most of the rank and file's legitimate grievances by providing proper leave, food, rest and

RIGHT: Three British commanders. From the left: General Sir Herbert Plumer (Second Army), General Sir Edmund Allenby (Third) and General Sir Henry Horne (First), February 1917. All three would distinguish themselves in the coming battles.

Underground Warfare: The Tunnels of Messines

Ever since antiquity, siege warfare has depended on the ability of engineers to construct elaborate trench and tunnel systems, and as the war on the Western Front resembled an enormous siege, it was almost inevitable that the tunnelers should come to the fore. The Germans were the first exponents of defensive underground systems, which so surprised the British on the Somme, and developed into the subterranean cities of the Hindenburg Line. The Allies, particularly Britain, correspondingly pioneered offensive underground techniques which included the construction of huge caverns near the front line for hiding and protecting troops prior to 'going over the top.' However, it was in the construction of tunnels and underground mines that the British achieved their most spectacular results.

While the underlying geology prevented the use of tunnels in some areas, they were employed in the great battlefields of the Somme and Ypres. At first tunnels were relatively simple, dug beneath sections of the line where No Man's Land was reasonably close, their function being to collapse enemy trenches. The knowledge that the enemy was tunneling beneath one was, of course, highly disconcerting (and potentially fatal), but this kind of tunneling was of strictly limited importance. By 1916, however, the British were digging deeper and farther underneath the German lines to excavate very large mine chambers in order to blow enemy strongpoints in support of major offensives. These large underground mines had been employed with some success on the opening day of the Battle of the Somme, but it was in the ripping apart of Messines Ridge that the tunnelers came into their own.

Once the trenches had become permanent fighting positions, the Royal Engineers began to recruit and draft in men with mining experience (of which there were hundreds of thousands in this period) to form special tunneling companies; 21 had been formed by the end of 1915 and their numbers continued to expand as the war went on. The tunnelers were an elite force; their special skills and the exhausting nature of the work, combined with all the other horrors of war, gave them a unique position in the history of warfare on the Western Front.

Messines Ridge, running southward from the town of Ypres, was well-suited to mining operations and the infantry of the British Second Army were in need of every possible assistance if the attack was

to succeed. Of the 19 mines detonated on the morning of 7 June, some had been started over a year previously, such was the slow and painstaking work of military tunneling. Mechanical diggers had been tried, but were not a success; the diggers still relied on muscle power and the most effective workers were those men who had worked on the building of the London Underground system, the heavy clays of the Thames basin being similar to those encountered in the Ypres area.

The tunnel entrances were situated 300-400 yards behind the front line and consisted of vertical shafts sunk through the surface topsoil, past a layer of heavy brown clay followed by a semi-liquid 'slurry' into a thick seam of blue clay. At this depth the main (horizontal) galleries were then slowly dug forward toward the German lines, and once the appropriate position had been reached, a large chamber was excavated for the explosives. The size of these mines were extensive. Kruisstraat Number 3 mine had a gallery 2160 feet long and a main charge of 30,000 lb of ammonal. Altogether, just under a million pounds in weight of high explosive was placed in position before the battle got underway.

During the final stages of the tunneling operation, the Germans dug an extensive system of counter-tunnels in an attempt to locate and destroy the British tunnels – the men digging on the key Hill 60 tunnel could hear the Germans getting closer and closer, but not close enough to stop the mines being blown on schedule at 0310 hours on 7 June. The detonation was a total success and the effect staggering – an earthquake that could be heard in London. The whole ground shook for miles around. On the ridge a British soldier observed: 'The earth opened and a large black mass mounted on pillars of fire reached into the sky, where it seemed to remain suspended for some seconds while an awful red glow lit up the surrounding desolation.'

Many Germans were killed outright, many were wounded and more still left in a state of dazed incomprehension by this terrifying ordeal. Advancing British troops noted the bewildered and numbed faces of the survivors, too shocked either to fight or run. The craters left by the explosives were enormous: the Spanbroekmolen crater was a gaping hole 250 feet wide, with a 'diameter of obliteration' of 430 feet – big enough to swallow up whole units of men. Messines was a triumphant vindication of the tactic of precise application of devastating firepower.

improved medical services. By late August the French Army was restored to a state of discipline and was able to mount an effective limited attack at Verdun, followed by another in Champagne in October. However, the mutinies made it necessary for the British Army to assume the main burden of the war in the West.

Senior British officers had long since concluded that the most rewarding area for a British offensive was Flanders; indeed, they would have preferred it to the Somme in 1916. The severe shipping losses of April and May now drew the attention of the Admiralty and the government toward the U-boat bases at Ostend and Zeebrugge, their elimination seemed vital if Britain was to survive. The chief action of the BEF in 1917 was thus shaped by the double objective of clearing the Flanders coast and forcing the Germans out of western Flanders altogether by cutting their rail communications in the neighborhood of Roulers, northeast of Ypres. Such a success would have the further advantage of ending the stalemate in the notorious and costly Ypres salient.

The first stage of a Flanders offensive had to be the securing of Ypres by capturing the Messines Ridge south of the town. Preparations for this had begun a year earlier with the digging of mines under the ridge. The tunneling companies of General Sir Herbert Plumer's Second Army had now completed 19 mines containing around a million pounds of high explosive in total. Although Plumer resembled the archetypal 'Colonel Blimp,' complete with white walrus mustache and rubicund features, he was arguably the most thoughtful British army commander of the war. He was well aware of the siege-warfare nature of the fighting on the Western Front and he planned his offensives accordingly, with meticulous detail. He was lucky to be served by an excellent Chief of Staff, Lieutenant General Sir Charles Harrington, who translated his superior's ideas into manageable operational orders. Plumer's avowedly cautious approach saved lives and he earned the affectionate respect of the Second Army troops. His nickname – 'Daddy' Plumer – compared tellingly with that of General Sir Hubert Gough, the Fifth Army's thrusting commander who was known to many as the 'Butcher.'

Plumer's attack at Messines on 7 June opened with the explosion of the mines, causing a virtual earthquake, followed immediately by a hurricane bombardment of over 2000 guns. The infantry advance of nine divisions was a

RIGHT: The infamous Flanders mud holds fast an 18-pounder field gun, Zillebeke, 9 August 1917. The heavy rains of August would make conditions far worse than this, bringing movement of wheeled vehicles to a dead halt.

BELOW: Men of the Inniskilling Fusiliers display captured German souvenirs following the British victory on Messines Ridge, June 1917. The German objects include Maxim machine guns, bayonets, rifles, entrenching tools, steel helmets and, the most prized of all, ceremonial Pickelhaube helmets (here without the distinctive 'spike').

complete success; the ridge was taken according to plan and counterattacks were easily repelled. It was a triumph for the Second Army. Haig now transferred the main attack northward to Gough's Fifth Army, while also preparing an amphibious operation under Rawlinson to take Ostend. Preparations for these operations took a long time and upset the momentum of the offensive, allowing the Germans to shore up their defenses around Ypres. And as the British had improved their assault tactics by 1917, so too had the Germans developed their defensive techniques. Flexible defense was now standard practice in the German Army and good use was made of reinforced concrete pillboxes to create a series of interlocking strongpoints situated in the forward line. The Germans anticipated that most would survive the preliminary bombardment (unless hit by a large-caliber shell) and would then have to be neutralized by the infantry, slowly and with much loss of life.

In the end the amphibious attack was abandoned and Gough's first step postponed until 31 July, just in time to founder in an unusually wet August. Against the mud and the concrete pill-box defenses, Gough's men suffered intense misery and achieved little. Belatedly Haig turned again to Plumer, but this only caused further delay.

Plumer's methodical preparations were completed by 20 September, when the first of three step-by-step limited advances took place. Each was a triumphant success in good weather spearheaded by Australians and New Zealanders. The third, at Broodseinde on 4 October, was especially punishing for the Germans. A British breakthrough seemed imminent, German morale was at a low ebb and reserves were few. Plumer planned further efforts

along similar lines but on 7 October the weather turned cold and wet, and the battle slowly foundered in a sea of mud in which guns, mules and even wounded men sank without trace. The last advance, on 6 November, resulted in the capture by the Canadians of a brick-colored stain in the mud which had once been the village of Passchendaele, the ruin which gave the battle its name. The offensive ended on 12 November by which time British casualties had mounted to some 245,000 (plus 8500 French). German losses are not recorded; in all probability they almost equaled those of the attackers and it is significant that they called Passchendaele 'the greatest martyrdom of the war.'

While the Flanders battle raged the Germans stripped the remainder of their front in the West to the minimum. Taking advantage of this, the French attack in Champagne on 23 October captured over 11,000 prisoners. Elsewhere, however, October ended badly for the Allies. Italy had fought two hard battles of attrition: the Tenth Battle of the Isonzo in May (157,000 men lost in just over three weeks) and the Eleventh Battle from 18 August to 12 September (165,000 casualties). The Italian Army was badly weakened. Altogether, the 11 battles along the Isonzo resulted in over 600,000 Italian battlefield casualties for pitiful territorial gains.

On the other side of the mountains the Austrian generals were deeply pessimistic about the ability of their troops to withstand further offensives and made repeated requests to the Germans for help to mount an offensive of their own. Under the command of the highly experienced General Otto von Below, the Austro-German Fourteenth Army was created, comprising 16 divisions of which

ABOVE LEFT: A letter from the Western Front.

ABOVE: A battery of Australian heavy or 'siege' artillery is made ready for action in the Ypres sector, 12 September 1917. These 8-inch howitzers would be responsible for the smashing up of the delicate Flanders' drainage system.

ABOVE RIGHT: Austrian troops rest in a heavily sandbagged strongpoint in the Alpine foothills near the Piave River.

RIGHT: Both 9.2-inch howitzers await the order to fire. They have been sited in a rather exposed position by Guillemont, 4 October 1917.

seven were German. Maintaining great secrecy, the Fourteenth Army was assembled and deployed along the Isonzo battlefront in early October and last-minute preparations were made for the battle which was later named after one of its focal points, the village of Caporetto.

A short whirlwind bombardment announced the opening of the attack on 24 October. Crack Austrian and German mountain units, pressing forward through snowstorms and low cloud, tore the Italian defenses apart. Communications broke down and the Italian Army collapsed with hundreds of thousands of men deserting and 275,000 surrendering. Battle casualties numbered only 40,000, and 2500 guns were captured. The Italian retreat continued to the Piave River some 60 miles from Caporetto. Here the men were able to stand on prepared positions against the now exhausted Austro-Germans while six French and five British divisions came to their support from the Western Front. By 12 November the fighting was over; it had delivered a severe and shocking blow to Allied hopes of outright victory.

The Battle of Third Ypres

Better known to the troops who fought there as Passchendaele, Third Ypres was the major British offensive of 1917. The British High Command was generally optimistic and expected significant results, and although a body blow was dealt to the German Army, the British Army also suffered badly. Passchendaele knocked away some of the army's confidence; the idea of a great military victory disappeared and from then on the war was a question of grimly hanging on until one side gave way.

Apart from the heavy casualties (245,000 men) and the loss of hope engendered by the battle, the physical conditions were atrocious. The heavy rainfall and repeated artillery bombardment turned the Ypres region into a vast, featureless quagmire: at its worst it was too soft to stand on, too thin to swim in, but sufficient to drown a man. The horrors of the mud became a recurring theme:

It was an absolute nightmare. Often we would have to stop and wait for up to half an hour, because all the time the duckboards were being blown up and men being blown off the track or simply slipping off ... We were loaded like Christmas trees, so of course an explosion nearby or just the slightest thing would knock a man off balance and he would go off the track and right down, into the muck.

LIEUTENANT P KING,
East Lancashire Regiment.

We heard screaming coming from a crater a bit away. I went over to investigate with a couple of the lads. It was a big hole and there was a fellow of the 8th Suffolks in it up to his shoulders. So I said, 'Get your rifles, one man in the middle to stretch them out, make a chain and let him get hold of it.' But it was no use. It was too far to stretch, we couldn't get any force on it, and the more we pulled and the more he struggled the further he seemed to go down. He went down gradually. He kept begging us to shoot him. But we couldn't shoot him. Who could shoot him? We stayed with him, watching him go down in the mud. And he died. He wasn't the only one. There must have been thousands up there who died in the mud.

SERGEANT T BERRY DCM,
The Rifle Brigade

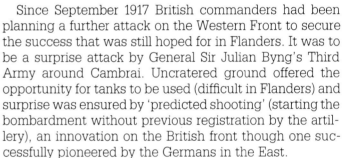

Since September 1917 British commanders had been planning a further attack on the Western Front to secure the success that was still hoped for in Flanders. It was to be a surprise attack by General Sir Julian Byng's Third Army around Cambrai. Uncratered ground offered the opportunity for tanks to be used (difficult in Flanders) and surprise was ensured by 'predicted shooting' (starting the bombardment without previous registration by the artillery), an innovation on the British front though one successfully pioneered by the Germans in the East.

At 0620 hours on 20 November, 1000 guns opened fire with a single crash on the unsuspecting Germans and 378 fighting tanks rolled forward through the mist. By midday the British had penetrated some four miles through the forward defenses of the Hindenburg Line. However, the cavalry failed to exploit the success and the Germans continued to hold strong positions on the flanks of the British advance. Furthermore, half the tanks were out of action at the end of the day largely due to mechanical failure. Yet another battle had degenerated into trench-to-trench fighting for which the British had no reserves (five divisions having gone to Italy).

On 30 November it was the turn of the Germans to spring a surprise in the form of a counterattack spearheaded by 'storm troops.' These specially trained groups used the tactics of 'infiltration' to find and exploit the weak points of the British line and then dislocate it with deep penetrations and encirclements. This marked the debut of the tactic on the Western Front and, like the British combination of predicted shooting and tanks, it worked well. The British were caught off-balance by the brilliantly executed German attack. The 12th and 55th Divisions were swept away by the German storm troops and the retreat was only prevented from becoming a rout by the arrival of steadfast reinforcements, notably the Guards Division. By 5 December, when the battle ended, the British had lost most of their territorial gains and both sides had suffered about 45,000 casualties.

ABOVE LEFT: *A group of less than dispirited Italian prisoners prepare for captivity for the 'duration' following their capture in the Battle of Caporetto, October 1917.*

LEFT: *The Battle of Cambrai, November 1917 – British troops file up a neatly dug German communication trench.*

ABOVE: *Although it was through their success as an infantry support weapon that the tanks gained their reputation at Cambrai, they had other uses as indicated here – a tank brings back a captured long-barreled 15cm field gun.*

RIGHT: *A machine-gun team of the 11th Leicester Regiment takes over a captured second-line trench at Ribecourt near Cambrai, 20 November 1917. These positions would soon be lost to a German counterattack at the end of the month, taking the gloss off the initial victory.*

Tank Development

Owing much to the enthusiastic intervention of Winston Churchill, the idea of armored landships began to take shape in early 1915. Experiments were carried out with a variety of designs, the most successful evolving through the caterpillar-tracked 'Little Willie' into 'Mother.' The prototype for the Tank Mk I (the name derived from the codename 'water tank'), 'Mother' was immediately recognizable through its distinctive lozenge-shaped tracks and the sponsons on each side of the tank, each mounting a six-pounder gun. During 1916 further modifications were made, including the division of 'male' tanks (armed with six-pounders) and 'female' (armed with machine guns).

Reliability and mobility were major problems with the Mk I but the military were keen to use tanks in action, and so a delivery to France was planned to allow them to take part in one of the forthcoming Somme offensives. Although fewer tanks arrived than originally promised, the Battle of Flers-Courcelette on 15 September 1916 was distinguished by the debut of tanks. They certainly surprised the Germans and achieved dramatic local successes, but by the end of the first day's fighting, almost all the 50 tanks originally deployed were inoperable, the majority having broken down.

In the light of battlefield experience and further developments, by the summer of 1917 the improved Mk IV was coming into production (only a few Mk IIs and Mk IIIs were built). It was the Mk IV tank which spearheaded the advance at Cambrai and played a vital role in the great British offensives of 1918. Capable of a top road speed of three-and-a-half miles per hour (half that in cross-country conditions), it was still desperately slow, generally hard to maneuver and unreliable. Yet the suc-cess of the attacks at Cambrai in November 1917 and at Amiens on 8 August 1918 revealed the tank's potential.

The Mk V tanks saw service toward the end of the war and represented a general upgrading of the Mk IV. An interesting development of 1918 was the introduction of the Medium Tank A or Whippet. Capable of a maximum speed of eight miles per hour the Whippet was designed to act in a cavalry role, exploiting army break-throughs in the enemy line. This they did with considerable success in the offensive battles of the summer and fall of 1918, some achieving deeper penetrations behind enemy lines and creating havoc wherever they went.

The French too were quick to see the potential of the tank and developed a number of models during the course of the war. The Char d'Assault Schneider was an early, and largely unsuccessful, model but was followed by the Char d'Assault St Chamond which was armed with a forward-firing 75mm gun. The most successful French design was the Renault FT17, a light tank produced in great numbers and armed with a turret-mounted 37mm gun or machine guns. By the end of the war there were about 2000 FT17s in service, some of which had been handed over to the Americans who used them alongside the heavy British Mk V.

The Germans, by contrast, were slow to take up the tank and, when they did use them, they usually employed captured British models. However, they did produce one tank design of their own, the lumbering 33-ton A7V. Crewed by 18 men the A7V was armed with a 5.7cm main gun and up to six machine guns. Cross-country performance was poor and, significantly, only 20 were produced before the end of the war.

The failure to win a decision in Flanders, the U-boat campaign, Russia's collapse, the heavy defeat of Italy and now the Cambrai setback meant a year of persistent disappointment ended gloomily for the Western Allies. However, profound war-weariness settled on all the combatant nations, soldiers and civilians alike. Despite all their best efforts, neither side seemed capable of achieving a decisive military victory but, as the war had gained its own momentum, disengagement was virtually impossible. Calls for peace had become more frequent during 1917 but the problems remained the same: what sort of peace and on whose terms? Given the titanic expenditure of men and materiel, no country was prepared to accept a negotiated peace based on the acceptance of a pre-1914 status quo. Each nation felt it deserved some sort of 'return' for such enormous investments of national resources in the war.

In January 1916 Colonel House, the US President's powerful roving envoy, made an attempt to sound out the war aims of the opposing sides and what peace terms they would demand or accept. United States mediation

LEFT: *British tanks – used en* masse *for the first time at Cambrai – overwhelmed the German frontline defenders, and the speed of the British advance took the commanders of both sides by surprise. However, the Germans were quick to recover from their early discomfiture.*

BELOW LEFT: *The tanks of World War I had many problems, mainly relating to reliability, although their intrinsic unmaneuverability made them vulnerable to rough terrain. This tank was knocked out of the battle by falling into a shell hole.*

RIGHT: *A German supply column stops alongside wounded troops while moving up toward the front near Armentières.*

BELOW: *British tanks await dispatch to forward detraining railheads in preparation for the Cambrai offensive.*

soon foundered on the rocks of mutual national intransigence. Moreover, while the 'doves' were deeply divided on what constituted acceptable terms for peace, the 'hawks' were united in their determination to pursue the war until it was won (or lost) by military action alone. By 1917 the 'hawks' held most of the key positions: Lloyd George as Prime Minister of a coalition government; the fiery, anti-German Georges Clemenceau had become President of France, and Ludendorff and Hindenburg had assumed dictatorial powers in Germany. For men like these, there could be only one objective: outright victory. The war would continue.

CHAPTER EIGHT

THE WAR IN THE AIR

On 17 December 1903 the Wright Brothers coaxed their fragile flying machine into the sky and made the first heavier-than-air flight in history. Less than eight years later (1 November 1911), an Italian military aviator dropped four grenades on Turkish troops during the war in Libya – the first hostile action in what would become a new type of warfare. Three years later the nations of Europe were locked in battle, each possessing small but expanding aviation branches. Military aviation was in its infancy at the outbreak of war, but it was quick to learn. A remarkably swift and complete assimilation of technological change meant that by the end of the war the new air forces had risen to semi-autonomous positions alongside the navies and the armies of the leading military powers. In the years leading up to the outbreak of war in 1914, the armed services had been experimenting with the possibilities of aircraft, although their overall usefulness and performance remained in question.

Thus while some officers were keen proponents of the aircraft as a weapon of war (such as General Grierson, commander of the British II Corps when war broke out), others were wholly dismissive, an attitude articulated by General Foch after watching an aerial performance: 'That is good sport but for the Army the aeroplane is useless.'

The Germans showed an additional interest in the airship, popularly dubbed the Zeppelin after its inventor, and had five available for service in the West in August 1914. The German Army made poor use of the Zeppelins, however. One airship, Z-6, was foolishly sent to drop shells on the Belgian fortress of Liège on 5 August, following the initial failure of heavy artillery to destroy the fortifications. The few shells dropped by the Zeppelin had no appreciable effect on the Belgian position, but the airship was badly holed by Belgian fire and finally wrecked during a forced landing near Bonn. Thereafter the Army showed

little interest in the Zeppelin until the Navy scored a sensational success in the bombing of England. The German High Command also failed to appreciate the potential of heavier-than-air machines. The German aviation service was poorly prepared for the war, its machines obsolescent compared to those in French and British service, and it was poorly directed during the great battles of 1914. Only in 1915 did German aviators make an important contribution to the air war.

The armies of 1914 consisted of millions of men operating across entire countries and, because communications were still primitive, a commander's ability to control and order his own men while discerning the presence and intentions of the enemy was of paramount importance. Reconnaissance was the responsibility of the cavalry but by 1914 the material requirements of finding out the enemy's dispositions were beyond the physical capabilities of the horse. On the other hand, the airplane of 1914 was capable of speeds of over 60mph, an endurance time of up to three hours and, from its vantage point in the sky, could see for miles around. Indeed, it was the pilots of the British RFC (Royal Flying Corps) and the French Air Service who spotted the German First Army's famous change of direction before Paris which led to the Battle of the Marne. Information of this quality helped shine a light through the 'fog of war,' liberating the generals (if only to a degree) from its crippling effect. At sea the aircraft's ability to look over the horizon was extremely valuable, however, and partly because of this both the German and British Navies encouraged their aviation branches, which tended to be more progressive and adventurous in outlook than their army counterparts.

Once the reconnaissance or scout aircraft was established as a regular feature over the battlefield, obvious countermeasures began to be applied; thus the need for

PREVIOUS PAGES: A squadron of the newly formed RAF (only four months old when this picture was taken in August 1918) lines up in preparation for a flight over enemy lines.

ABOVE: Captain Oswald Boelcke, one of the 'Eindecken' aces.

ABOVE RIGHT: Lieutenant Max Immelman, one of the first aces and a pioneer fighter pilot.

BELOW: An early World War I photograph designed to show interservice co-operation – a Maurice Farman 'Longhorn' flies over French infantry holding a hastily dug trench.

ABOVE: Standing in front of his personalized Spad, Lieutenant Georges Guynemer was an early member of the French 'Storks' Squadron.

BELOW: An early British fighter-reconnaissance biplane.

information was balanced by the need to deny it to the enemy. At first the crews of the opposing machines merely waved to each other to acknowledge contact, but this innocent chivalry quickly faded with the arrival of revolvers, shotguns and rifles in the cockpit. In these primitive attempts to arm the aircraft lay the genesis of the 'fighter' and the concept of air superiority. The first plane to be downed was an old German Taube which was forced to land behind Allied lines by three RFC aircraft on 25 August 1914.

The Germans and the French led the race to transform the observation platform into a fighter. The obvious aircraft weapon was a flexibly mounted forward-firing machine gun. Some aircraft, mainly early models, were of the 'pusher' type in which the propeller was fitted at the rear of the fuselage, thereby pushing the aircraft forward; these could be easily adapted to take a machine gun. Most aircraft, however, were of the 'tractor' type, with the propeller mounted conventionally at the forward end of the fuselage. Thus, any bullets fired directly forward would shoot off the propeller, and a wide field of fire was taken up by the propeller's arc of movement.

The solution to 'firing' through the airscrew was a two-stage process. In February 1915 the French team of Roland Garros and Raymond Saulnier fitted steel deflector plates to the propeller to ensure that its blades were not shot away, although most of the bullets (around 93 percent) were anyway fired into the 'gaps' between the rotating blades. Garros shot down several German aircraft before being shot down himself in April 1915. The Germans inspected his aircraft and improved it by developing the more sophisticated interrupter gear system in which, through a geared linkage system, the machine gun did not fire at the moment the propeller passed in front of it. The talented Dutch aviation designer Anthony Fokker com-

bined the interrupter gear system with his own Fokker monoplane which, in its E-III version, was arguably the world's first true fighter aircraft.

In the hands of experienced pilots such as Max Immelmann and Oswald Boelcke, the Fokker played havoc with the slow-moving aircraft of the Allies in what became known as the 'Fokker Scourge.' These skilled and ruthless fliers who roamed the skies over France and Flanders in search of victims gained an enthusiastic following among the civilian population. Their careers were closely followed in the popular press and their inevitable deaths caused widespread mourning. Whereas the foot soldiers were bogged down in a muddy war of attrition, these young pilots represented all that was glamorous in war and were glorified as latter-day 'knights of the air.' The great battles on the Western Front lacked easily discernible results and were hard for the public to comprehend.

All the major combatant nations produced great fighter pilots. The French grouped many of their best pilots into the famous *Les Cigognes* (Storks) Squadron which included the extraordinary Georges Guynemer (54 kills). Despite frequently being shot down he continued to fly at every opportunity even though his health was poor and the government had requested he quit the service. The top-scoring French pilot of the war, René Fonck (75 kills), was also a *Cigognes* member and an outstanding marksman, capable of shooting down an opponent with a few well-placed rounds. On two occasions he destroyed five German aircraft in a day.

The Germans also created elite fighter units, the most famous being *Jagdgeschwader I* commanded by the top-scoring war ace Baron Manfred von Richthofen (80 kills) and better known as Richthofen's Flying Circus. As the first nation to develop an effective fighter aircraft, the Germans pioneered aerial tactics which included such ruses

ABOVE: Pilots of Richthofen's own pursuit flight on the Western Front.

RIGHT: Captain René Fonck practising scoring bullseyes at 25 yards with a carbine.

BELOW: The clean-cut personification of the British air ace, Captain Albert Ball.

BOTTOM: The ace of aces, Manfred von Richthofen with 80 victories to his credit.

BELOW RIGHT: A line of Albatross fighters of Richthofen's circus.

BELOW, FAR RIGHT: Sopwith triplanes of a naval squadron. They were the influence behind the famous Fokker triplane.

as attacking enemy aircraft from out of the sun ('Beware the Hun in the Sun' was a famous RFC saying). The Germans also fought in pairs for mutual support and introduced a whole range of specialized flying techniques designed to bring down an adversary. The Immelmann Turn was one of the most famous of these tactics, a maneuver which allowed an aircraft to maintain height while turning. Immelmann and Oswald Boelcke were the two great first-generation German aces clocking up 15 and 40 kills respectively, and both were early victims of the dogfight war. Other important German aces were Ernst Udet (62 kills) and Hermann Göring (22 kills), the latter taking over as commander of *Jagdgeschwader I* after Richthofen's death in April 1918, and later becoming infamous as Hitler's deputy.

Unlike the French and Germans, the British officially disapproved of the ace system (technically, five or sometimes 10 aerial victories) although, in fact, they produced the largest number of aces. Perhaps the most talented was Albert Ball (44 kills), who died before the age of 21 and epitomized the spirit of the air ace. Shortly before he was shot down in May 1917, Ball summed up his feelings: 'Oh, it was a good fight, and the Huns were fine sports. One tried to ram me, after he was hit, and only missed me by inches. Am indeed looked after by God, but Oh! I do get tired of living always to kill and am really beginning to feel like a murderer. I shall be so pleased when I have finished.'

The strain placed on these men was immense and for most pilots every combat patrol was a private battle between fear and the call of duty, a combination which so often proved fatal. Some managed to transcend these human frailties and it was the quality of unbounded self-confidence that distinguished the great aces. One of the most notable was Edward Mannock whose final score of 73 kills made him the top British ace. Beside his extraordinary flying talent, Mannock was a most able commander (most aces were essentially loners) and was highly regarded by almost all who served under him.

From the other nations, the Austrian ace Godwin Brumowski achieved 40 kills, mostly on the Italian Front; the Belgian Willy Coppens scored 37, 28 of which were observation balloons – far from easy targets; Francesco Baracca shot down 34 enemy aircraft for Italy and, of the American aces, Edward Rickenbacker scored highest with 26 kills, all achieved in a mere four months during 1918. Many Americans had served in the French Air Service before the United States' entry into the war and had been brigaded

TOP: *The highly maneuverable Sopwith Camel, the top-scoring fighter of any side during the war.*

ABOVE: *The French Nieuport XVII was another fine scout aircraft.*

LEFT: *Raoul Lufbery, an American in the French Lafayette Squadron.*

together in the Lafayette Squadron which included star pilots like Raoul Lufbery, a natural flier who shot down 17 aircraft before his own death in combat.

By 1917, however, organized formation flying had begun to take over from the lone patrols of the 'knights of the air.' Large and tightly formed groups of aircraft could provide good mutual protection and effectively overwhelm the flying skills of the fighter aces. If this marked the end of a golden age of chivalry, it also heralded a new sense of professionalism in combat flying. Although organization was a vital factor in the race for aerial supremacy, just as important was the quality of aircraft available to each side. The air force which possessed the best aircraft at any given time could virtually guarantee air superiority over the Western Front.

Air supremacy swung from one side to the other as aviation developed. The German superiority of 1915 and early 1916 was countered by the arrival of better Allied aircraft, notably the French Nieuport XVII and the British DH2. In September the first twin-gunned Albatross fighters were deployed in the German Air Service, and proceeded to overwhelm the Allies that autumn and the following spring. By April 1917 – 'Bloody April' – the RFC was at its lowest ebb. The life expectancy of young, inexperienced pilots was only a few days, and morale began to fall. At this point a new generation of British aircraft – the Sopwith Triplane, the SE5/SE5a and the Sopwith Camel, among others – turned the tables in favor of the Allies. Only in the last months of the war did the Germans look like regaining the initiative with the introduction of the Fokker DVII, but they were too few in numbers to turn the tide.

While the 'dogfighting' exploits of the fighter aces captured the imagination of the public the primary role of

Mick Mannock: Ace

One of the great Allied fighter pilots of the war was Major Edward 'Mick' Mannock. Britain's top ace (73 kills) and a superb flight commander. This account by a close comrade helps explain the 'how' and 'why' of a legend:

In his first fight, which commenced at 12,000 feet, there were six Pfalz scouts flying east from Kemmel Hill direction. One he shot to pieces after firing a long burst from directly behind and above; another he crashed; it spun into the ground after it had been hit by a deflection shot; the other, a silverbird, he had a fine set-to with, while his patrol watched the master at work. It was a wonderful sight. First they waltzed around one another like a couple of turkey-cocks, Mick being tight on his adversary's tail. Then the Pfalz half-rolled and fell a few hundred feet beneath him. Mick followed, firing as soon as he got in position. The Hun then looped – Mick looped too, coming out behind and above his opponent and firing short bursts. The Pfalz then spun – Mick spun also, firing as he spun. This shooting appeared to me a waste of ammunition. The Hun eventually pulled out; Mick was fast on his tail – they were now down to 400 feet. The Pfalz now started twisting and turning which was a sure sign of 'wind-up.' After a sharp blunt close up, Mick administered the *coup de grace*, and the poor old fellow went down headlong and crashed.

This was a really remarkable exhibition of cruel, cool, calculating Hun-strafing. A marvelous show. I felt sorry for the poor Hun, for he put up a wonderful show of defensive fighting. His

effort reminded me of mine on 12 April. The only difference was that he was miles over his own lines and had a slower machine. Had he only kept spinning down to the ground, I think he would have got away with it.

I asked Mick after we landed why he fired during the spin. 'He replied, 'Just to intensify his wind-up.' And a very good answer, too! This was the first occasion that I have seen a machine loop during a fight. It was obvious to us watching that to loop under such circumstances is foolish. Mick managed, however, to keep behind him, though, and did not lose contact with him although it was obvious by his maneuvers after he came out of the loop that the Pfalz pilot was all at sea, for he twisted and turned his machine in a series of erratic jerks just as if he was a dog stung on his tail! Mick says he only looped as well for a bit of fun as he felt his opponent was 'cold meat.' He says what he should have done instead of looping was to have made a zooming climbing turn as the Pfalz looped, then half-rolled and come back on his tail as he came out of the loop. By this means he would have been able to keep the Hun in sight all the time, while he would not have lost control of his machine as the Hun did while coming out of the loop.

Mick's other Hun was a Hannoveranner two-seater which he shot down after a burst at right angles. The old boy crashed into a tree near La Couronne, south of Vieux. Four in one day! What is the secret? Undoubtedly the gift of accurate shooting combined with determination to get to close quarters before firing.

Major Edward 'Mick' Mannock, the top British ace.

LEFT: *German reconnaissance aircraft at the Battle of Marne in 1914.*

RIGHT: *A German Gotha heavy bomber returns from a long-range night mission over England. These attacks marked the beginnings of strategic bombing.*

FAR RIGHT: *German Junkers ground-attack aircraft come under fire from British aircraft, but are protected by a German fighter escort. This scene demonstrates the rapid progress of aerial tactical development during the course of the war.*

BELOW: *The Albatross DVa, the scourge of the Allied air forces in the spring of 1917, was greatly superior to any French or British aircraft.*

BELOW RIGHT: *A somewhat lurid picture of a German Fokker DV11 shooting down an Allied Spad.*

BELOW, FAR RIGHT: *A fairly typical dogfight painting of the era – the painter is German and so it is an Allied aircraft that is shot down in flames.*

craft throughout the war was to support the ground forces. In trench warfare dominated by artillery, the airmen played a vital part in observing enemy entrenchments, artillery batteries, machine-gun positions and other sites in the rear. Photographic reconnaissance was soon introduced, enabling the minutest details to be incorporated on trench and artillery maps. Air-to-ground communications developed steadily, especially between artillery batteries and spotting aircraft which located enemy gun positions and guided the gunners' fall of shot onto the target.

The advances in air warfare originated mainly on the Western Front, but aerial activity was not confined to that theater. The Russians experimented (with limited success) with four-engined bombers, and warplanes from Italy and Austria-Hungary flew and fought over the Alps and Adriatic Sea. In Palestine during 1918, General Allenby's air force turned the Turkish retreat into a rout. At sea, air observation had become a regular feature and experimental aircraft carriers were introduced near the end of the war. Airships, seaplanes and conventional aircraft all made a contribution to anti-submarine warfare.

The emergence of the aircraft as a multi-role fighting machine was completed with the development of the bomber. The Royal Naval Air Service (RNAS) was an early pioneer of strategic bombing, launching its first raid with an attack on Zeppelin sheds at Dusseldorf and Cologne on 22 September 1914. Some enterprising airmen had begun to carry simple missiles, such as ball-bearings or darts, to drop on the enemy; these were soon replaced by shells, grenades and bombs. Bomber aircraft progressed along two separate paths: in their tactical role they provided support for ground troops, strafing enemy formations with machine guns and anti-personnel bombs; their strategic function was to attack the enemy positions and industrial targets far behind the front line.

The early bomber aircraft not only lacked proper aerial bombs, but also bombsights. The latter arrived in 1915

TOP LEFT: An RFC ground crewman fits an aerial camera to the aircraft under his charge. Despite the exploits of the fighter aces, reconnaissance remained the single most important task of the aviation services.

ABOVE LEFT: An air mechanic hands over photographic plates to the observer of an RE8 for a mission over Arras, February 1918.

LEFT: An SE5 of No. 111 Squadron stationed in Palestine 1917-18. The SE5a was an excellent aircraft for the reconnaissance and fighter duties that it would have been expected to carry out in this theater of operations.

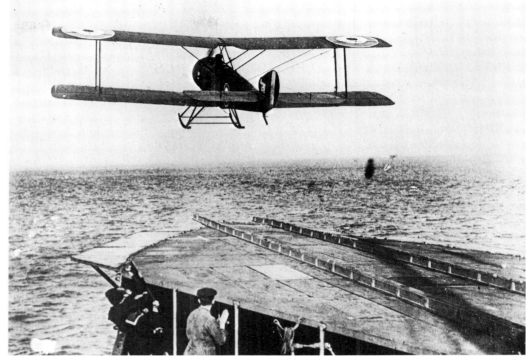

ABOVE: RFC officers make up a mosaic of photographs taken over German lines. These photographic maps provided up-to-date information on German movements and intentions for the troops on the ground.

ABOVE RIGHT: A Sopwith strutter takes off from an aircraft carrier – an example of the innovative ideas that came to fruition during the war.

RIGHT: A comparison of a single-seat fighter with a three-engined naval reconnaissance aircraft.

RIGHT: German aircrew kitted-out for protection against freezing winter temperatures.

FAR RIGHT: A wounded British pilot is led away by German troops.

LEFT: A convoy of German Zeppelins approaches England, bringing the war home to the British.

RIGHT: A Zeppelin flies over a German torpedo boat in home waters.

BELOW RIGHT: The exposed gondola of the German airship L6.

BELOW, FAR RIGHT: A diagram illustrating the course of several Zeppelin raids over London.

BELOW LEFT: A painting of the famous flight of L59 across Africa, seen here hovering over an oasis in the Sudan.

BELOW: A dramatic reconstruction of a Zeppelin bombing mission against London. Fires can be seen breaking out to the north and east of Tower Bridge.

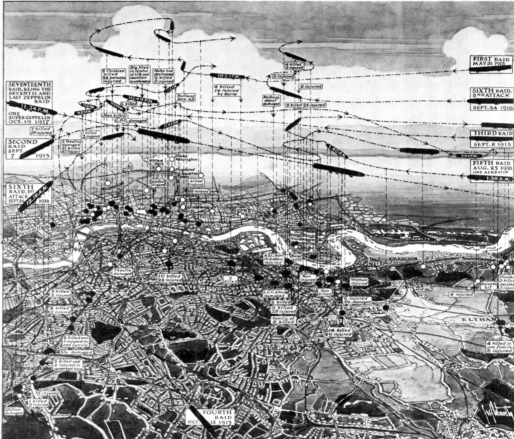

Death of a Zeppelin

The Zeppelin menace took the British air services a long time to master and caused grave concern to the British people, their island nation violated by an intruder for the first time in centuries. This Admiralty announcement of the first shooting down of a Zeppelin was greeted with national jubilation. The successful pilot, Warneford, received a VC for his endeavors:

At 3am this morning Flight Sub-Lieutenant R A J Warneford, RN, attacked a Zeppelin in the air between Ghent and Brussels at 6000 feet. He dropped six bombs, and the airship exploded, fell to the ground and burnt for a considerable time. The force of the explosion caused the Morane monoplane to turn upside down. The pilot succeeded in righting the machine, but had to make a forced landing in the enemy's country. However, he was able to restart his engine and returned safely to the aerodrome.

Admiralty announcement, 7 June 1915

when the RFC hit rail communications behind the German lines during the Battle of Loos. The RFC did not possess the necessary numbers of aircraft or the destructive weight of bombs to be really successful, but the raid nonetheless marked the first attempt at interdiction bombing.

The first real example of a strategic air offensive against a civilian population was made by Germany. Initially, Zeppelin airships were used but these were followed by specially designed long-range bombers. The first Zeppelin attack on England was launched on 19 January 1915 and this was followed by a further 19 raids during the year. Casualties were relatively light (a total of 556 dead and 1357 injured), but the public outcry was huge. England had lost its island security and immediate countermeasures were demanded. These were slow in coming, however, as the Zeppelins proved surprisingly hard to shoot down. It was 1916 before a defensive system of anti-

The Flight of L59

Of all the many daring exploits undertaken by Germany's Zeppelin crews, none was more audacious than that of L59's African adventure. In an attempt to supply the beleaguered forces of Colonel von Lettow-Vorbeck in German East Africa, the specially prepared L59 set off from Bulgaria on 21 November 1917 carrying a 13-ton cargo of essential military and medical supplies. During the night of the 21st, L59, commanded by Kapitan Leutnant Bockholt, began its crossing of the Mediterranean, and despite heavy storms which threatened to blow the airship off course, the African coastline was sighted early next morning. The L59's route took the airship well to the west of the Nile Valley, thus evading the British forces stationed there.

The high temperature and bad air turbulence caused the L59 severe difficulty in keeping a straight course across the desert, but the crew gradually mastered the techniques of desert flying and by the early hours of 23 November they were on a latitude parallel with Khartoum's – over half way to their destination. Then to Bockholt's dismay, he received a radio message ordering him to return to Bulgaria. British successes against Lettow-Vorbeck had convinced German intelligence that the East African garrison was beyond help. Reluctantly L59 turned for home, reaching its base in Bulgaria on 25 November having covered over 4000 miles. Although the flight of the L59 failed in its original supply mission, it was a triumph for the skills of Germany's elite Zeppelin crews. In addition, it provided a glimpse of the extraordinary intercontinental potential of the airship for civil aviation after World War I.

aircraft guns, searchlights, barrage balloons and night-fighters was brought into service.

The Germans began to phase out their Zeppelin raids in 1916, not so much in response to the British defenses, more because of the arrival of the superior Gotha and Giant airplanes. On 25 May 1917 Folkestone was bombed by Gothas, the first in a series of raids against southeast England over the next 12 months. Again casualties were few (a total of 835 killed and 1972 injured), but the outraged British public called for improved defensive measures and direct retaliation. An Independent Air Force (IAF) was created for the bombing of strategic targets in Germany, starting with the Handley Page series of bombers in 1918. The Handley Page 0/1500, with a range of nearly 1240 miles, was capable of reaching Berlin carrying 3300 pounds of bombs; only the armistice on 11 November 1918 prevented this true strategic bomber from demonstrating its capabilities.

The importance of aviation to the war was confirmed in Britain by the formation of a separate service – the Royal Air Force (RAF) on 1 April 1918. The growth of the RNAS, RFC and RAF since 1914 had been dramatic – from a handful of men and machines to a highly professional organization of 293,532 officers and men and 22,000 aircraft. By the end of the war it was the largest and most experienced air force in the world.

ABOVE: Crowds stare at bomb damage inflicted on the St John's Wood area of London, 7/8 March 1918. The 300kg bomb caused considerable damage and 15 casualties.

BELOW: The wreckage of German naval airship L33, destroyed over Little Wigborough on 23 September 1916.

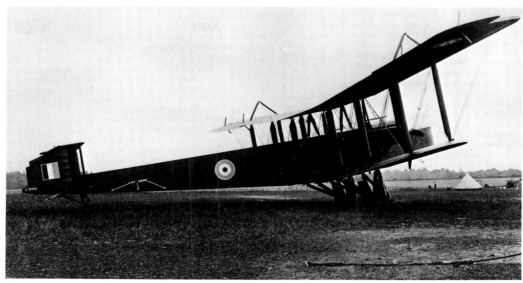

ABOVE: A German Zeppelin is maneuvered into its hangar at the conclusion of a mission.

ABOVE RIGHT: Britain's main heavy bomber of World War I, the Handley Page 0/400, had a maximum bombload of 2000lb and an armament of up to five Lewis guns.

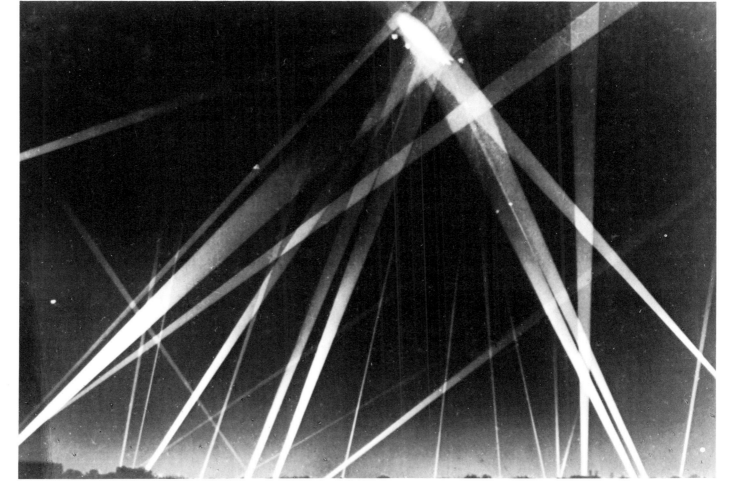

RIGHT: A German Zeppelin is thoroughly 'coned' by British searchlights operating throughout London. Anti-aircraft guns would then open up and were often followed by the arrival of nightfighters.

BELOW: The vast size of the Zeppelin can be appreciated in this aerial photograph of German airships and hangars.

CHAPTER NINE

RUSSIA IN TURMOIL

The German Army had inflicted a massive and costly defeat on Russia in the great summer offensive of 1915, and, as the German High Command turned its attention to the West in 1916, it was hoped that Russia would remain on the defensive. The Russian Army, even after 18 months of fighting, remained a cumbersome military machine led, in the main, by ill-educated generals with old-fashioned ideas on conducting a war. By 1916, however, there was some cause for optimism as Russia's industrial base finally began to expand. The chronic shortages of weapons, ammunition and other essential items of military equipment which had undermined Russian efforts in 1914-15 had largely been overcome by the spring of 1916. Conforming to the plans agreed between the Allies, the Russian High Command made preparations for renewed offensives on the Eastern Front.

Of all the Allied nations, Russia was the most responsive to pleas for help from others, as had been shown in the invasion of East Prussia in 1914 which was undertaken to ease pressure on the French during the critical period leading up to the Battle of the Marne. Again, it was a similar French request for a Russian offensive to draw German reserves away from their threatened Verdun sector which led to the ill-fated campaign around Lake Narotch. Two army groups were involved (the Northern Front under General A Kuropatkin and the Center Front under General Alexei Evert), with the important communications center of Vietna as their objective. The offensive was planned to open on 18 March.

As the Russians advanced round Lake Narotch, the spring thaw set in and the attack quickly bogged down. Strong German resistance guaranteed an unhappy end to this poorly prepared, quixotic Russian performance; the attacker's casualties numbered over 100,000 while those of the defenders were only a fifth of that figure. The battle-experienced German troops found little difficulty in repulsing offensives where the spearhead of the attack

PREVIOUS PAGES: Already under enemy fire, Russian troops slowly crawl toward barbed-wire entanglements.

LEFT: Although an overall defeat, Russian forces at Lake Narotch did score some localized successes including the capture of these German troops.

ABOVE: General Alexei Brusilov.

TOP: A Russian unit moves up to the front line.

ABOVE RIGHT: Russian troops crowd into a forward trench.

RIGHT: Armed with lances, German cavalry ride through a Russian village, January-February 1916.

still consisted of waves of Russian infantry as opposed to the heavy artillery barrages that were to become a regular feature on the Western Front. Although such a swift resurgence of offensive action by the Russians after the disaster of the previous year came as an unwelcome surprise to the Germans – as did their greatly increased stocks of artillery ammunition – the ease with which they stopped these attacks ('in mud and blood,' according to one German report) seemed to confirm their generally poor opinion of the Russian Army. They would soon be forced to revise this view.

At a major planning conference on 14 April 1916 attended by the Czar and his army group commanders, it was agreed to adopt an unorthodox offensive scheme put forward by General Alexei Brusilov, commanding the Southwest Army Group. His plan consisted of a wide-fronted advance that made maximum use of the element of surprise. Brusilov was one of the few Russian commanders who was at ease with the latest advances in military technology. Aerial photography, the construction of offensive trench systems, concealment of reserves and good artillery-infantry co-operation all played a part in his preparations for the attack.

On 4 June the four armies of Brusilov's Group (38 divisions against an Austro-German force of similar strength) attacked along a dispersed front of over 90 miles. Brusilov's careful preparations and tight pre-offensive security paid off, and the surprised Austro-German forces

ABOVE: The vast numbers of Austrian prisoners netted in the Brusilov Offensive stretched the Russian transport and logistical systems. Hardship was not unknown, although these prisoners seem to be in reasonable condition.

BELOW: General Erich von Falkenhayn. After his dismissal as Chief of Staff on 28 August 1916, he was given command of the operations against Rumania.

LEFT: Brusilov's Offensive, 1916.

fell back in disarray. As Brusilov had predicted the greatest successes came at the opposing ends of the Austrian line. In the south the Russian Ninth Army (General Letchitsky) crossed the Dniester River to the north of Czernowitz, flinging the Austrian Seventh Army (General Pfanzer-Baltkin) back against the Carpathian Mountains. In the north the Russian Eighth Army (General Kaledin) fared even better, smashing its way through the lines of the Austrian Fourth Army (Archduke Ferdinand), capturing the city of Lutsk in the process. Only in the center did the Austrian line hold – this section of the front included a number of German formations – but these troops were later forced to withdraw to conform with the retreat of the two wings.

The Russians pressed quickly forward: an advance of 60 miles by 12 June netted nearly 200,000 Austrian prisoners and vast stores of enemy equipment. At this point Brusilov needed support and strong reinforcements from his neighbors, but despite his entreaties for prompt action the response was slow. Yet again, German reinforcements arrived just in time to shore up a collapsing Austrian front. After a period of reorganization, Brusilov's Offensive was resumed in late July and August. By the beginning of September the Austrians had lost over 600,000 men and the Germans 150,000. Fighting continued during September (the peak of the Battle of the Somme) but, as Russian casualties mounted, the forward impetus of the advance could not be maintained and the attack slowly ground to a halt.

The Brusilov Offensive was a near-fatal blow to the Austro-Hungarian Empire. It also forced the German High Command to withdraw divisions from the Somme in the West, and also produced a new enemy for the Central Powers in the East. Encouraged by Allied promises of territory from Austria-Hungary and by the Russian success under Brusilov, Rumania declared war against Austria-Hungary on 27 August. This proved to be a fatal military error. Rumania's Army of 23 divisions was obsolete by 1916 standards, surrounded by enemies, and her strategic position was extremely vulnerable.

General Falkenhayn was dismissed as German Chief of Staff on 28 August and at once appointed commander of the combined Austro-German-Bulgarian operation against Rumania. He took direct command of the Austro-

German forces to the north of the country and soon revealed his ability as a field commander – even after two years spent as Germany's top staff officer. Rumania possessed no generals of similar energy and competence, however, as was soon made abundantly clear. Despite the fact that Bulgaria had joined her Austro-German partners for this campaign (with territorial objectives similar to those of the Serbian venture in 1915), the Rumanian Army persisted with its grandiose plan for an invasion of Austro-Hungarian territory over the Transylvanian Mountains, a considerable task even for large numbers of troops. A far more prudent plan would have been for Rumania to adopt an overall defensive policy in order to secure her southern borders from Bulgarian advances.

At first the Rumanian forces made some progress in pushing past the lightly held Austrian outposts in the Transylvanian Mountains, but by the end of September they had been forced back over the mountain passes. The Bulgarians (plus small German and Turkish contingents)

BELOW: A Rumanian gun crew rests during a bombardment. Ironically, their gun was supplied by Krupp of Germany and was the same model as that used by the German Army.

BOTTOM: Rumanian infantry cross a mountain river in the Transylvania region.

were led by another redoubtable German officer, August von Mackensen, and under his command they advanced into southeast Rumania, capturing Constanza, the country's chief port, and establishing bridgeheads over the River Danube by the end of October. Now in defense of their homeland, the Rumanians fought with an unexpected resilience but a swift German advance through the Vulcan Pass breached the Transylvanian defenses, forcing the Rumanians to fall back toward Bucharest. On 1 December Falkenhayn and Mackensen launched a coordinated attack against the Rumanians deployed in a loose ring around the capital city. Despite a determined Rumanian counterattack against the juncture of the armies of Falkenhayn and Mackensen which caused the Germans some problems, the outcome was never in serious doubt. At the end of the three-day battle the remnants of the Rumanian Army were retreating eastward, leaving behind 70,000 prisoners and Bucharest itself which opened its gates to the Germans on 6 December. Their own exhaustion and bad weather thwarted the Central Powers' close pursuit of the Rumanians, who were able to fall back on Moldavia and take up a new defensive position alongside the Russian Ninth Army. For minimal casualties the Germans had gained control of the country's important economic resources (oil and grain) for the benefit of a blockaded Germany.

The fall of Rumania forced an extension of the Russian line down to the Black Sea and was a further drain on the country's reserves of manpower. By the end of 1916 Russia's total casualties were estimated at around five million. Shortages of foodstuffs during the bitter winter of

ABOVE LEFT: *A German 21cm howitzer is sited within its emplacement ready for the assault on Rumanian positions at Sereth.*

ABOVE: *Rumanian dead lie scattered along a railway embankment, victims of the abortive offensive against Transylvania. The Rumanians were routed by German forces under General Falkenhayn.*

LEFT: *Promoted to the rank of Field Marshal, Mackensen inspects the troops that captured Bucharest in December 1916.*

RIGHT: *The great oil refinery at the Rumanian Black Sea port of Constanza is set afire, the flames visible for miles through the dense black clouds of smoke.*

1916-17 led to riots in the big cities and a growing revolutionary mood. In March 1917 mass demonstrations and strikes took place in many Russian cities. The basic slogans demanding food and an end to the war were beginning to acquire a new political dimension calling for the end of the Romanov dynasty. The 1905 Revolution had been suppressed by the unquestioning loyalty of the troops and police, but in March 1917 the troops began to fraternize with the demonstrators. The collapse of the old order was imminent.

On 12 March a disparate collection of opposition leaders, including members of the Russia Duma (parliament), socialists, revolutionaries, workers' leaders and politicized soldiers, set themselves up as the 'Provisional Government.' Czar Nicholas II, isolated and, following the defection of most of the Army and his bureaucracy, virtually powerless, accepted the inevitable and abdicated on 18 March. The new government, basically liberal in character, was committed to the continuation of the war and was at first expected to strengthen Russia's war effort. However, its authority was increasingly undermined by the activities of left-wing groups whose demands for 'peace and bread' met with a ready response from the war-weary Russian peasants and soldiers.

By 1917 war-weariness was not confined to Russia. Italy in just over eighteen months of war had suffered losses of about 750,000, and the mood of patriotic excitement with which the Italian public had greeted the war was fading. In France, apart from the army mutinies, there was a general feeling of demoralization on the home front as a series of traitorous scandals affecting government members came to light. In Britain the shock of conscription was added to the shocks of air bombardment and the food

The Czech Legion

Despite their membership of the Austro-Hungarian Empire, few Czechs had much sympathy for the regime, and once war had broken out in 1914 a growing (though still small) nationalist movement within Czechoslovakia began to look toward Slavic Russia for help in winning independence. In Russia itself there was a large Czech community – perhaps as many as 100,000 people – which had enthusiastically given its support to the war against Austria. The Russian reaction to this offer of help was mixed, but a battalion of Czechs (augmented by a few other nations) was raised during October 1914 and distinguished itself in the campaign in Galicia.

As the war progressed more Czechs joined the colors, while disgruntled Czech units in the Austro-Hungarian Army were encouraged to desert – and often did. The Russians were still mistrustful of the Czech force, however, and refused to allow them to recruit Czech prisoners. Also, understandable Czech frustration at Russia's refusal to accept the idea of an independent Czechoslovakia made matters worse. The 'February Revolution' in 1917 brought about a slight change in Russian policy, but it was only with the Bolshevik Revolution in November that the Czechs were given complete freedom to recruit as they chose and an under-strength division of 7000 men rapidly expanded to a full army corps of more than 30,000 men.

By 1916 Czech independence leaders led by Thomas Masaryk were based in France and had found the Western Allies most favorably disposed toward an autonomous Czech state. To strengthen the claim, Masaryk suggested that the Czechs should help by fighting on the Western Front. The French were keen on the plan and attempts were made to transport the Czechs to Western Europe during 1917, but in a Russia rapidly disintegrating into chaos they achieved little success.

As the Bolsheviks wanted an end to hostilities with the Germans, the reason for the existence of the Czech Army Corps in Russia evaporated. Masaryk, now in Russia, set about organizing the Czechs' departure which would be via the Trans-Siberian Railway and the Pacific port of Vladivostok. An agreement with the Soviet government was achieved and in March 1918 the Czechs began the move east. Progress was slow and by May the Czech Army Corps was strung out along the Trans-Siberian Railway. Relations with the Bolsheviks began to sour as both sides became increasingly antagonistic toward each other. A relatively minor incident on 14 May in the Siberian town of Chelyabinsk escalated into outright conflict, and the armed and well-organized Czechs had little difficulty in overcoming the Bolsheviks. By the end of June they had control of a long stretch of the railway – and the towns alongside – and were invovled in a number of skirmishes with the Bolsheviks.

The Czechs met up with Allied contingents at Vladivostok but a shortage of shipping prevented their evacuation. This, however, was a deliberate policy adopted by the Allies. With the war won in the West the Czechs would be more useful in Russia. The Allied interventionists hoped the Czechs would work alongside the anti-Bolshevik White Russian forces, but such an alliance proved desultory and throughout 1919 the Czechs remained in place, guarding their positions along the Trans-Siberian Railway. Although far from their intended destination in France, the Czech Legion's well-publicized exploits gave Masaryk and his fellow nationalist leaders a good bargaining lever during the Versailles Peace Treaty negotiations. Finally, in February 1920 – with the Russian Civil War decided in favor of the Bolsheviks – the Czechs were shipped out from Vladivostock. They steamed back toward a new Europe with an independent Czechoslovakia – a state which, even if indirectly, they had helped create. The struggle of the Czech Legion did not, however, have any long-term effect on the outcome of World War I.

shortages due to submarine blockade. The International Socialist Conference in Stockholm in June provided a focus for discontent, but Russia's example was the most important stimulus for subsequent action.

The Western Allies were reassured by the avowed determination of the Provisional Government to carry on the war. The deposition of the Czar was considered in a favorable light by many liberals in the Allied camp. The war could now be seen as a moral crusade of the parliamentary democracies, representing all that was good and progressive, against the reactionary and autocratic regimes of the Central Powers. This was a useful argument for the pro-war faction in America, which was anyway poised to declare war on Germany on account of the unrestricted submarine warfare campaign. Now that the centuries-old Romanov dynasty had gone for ever, liberals could claim they were fighting 'to make the world safe for democracy' – as the words of a contemporary slogan put

ABOVE LEFT: One of the many political marches that took place in Petrograd in 1917 – a commemoration of the dead who fell in the revolution.

ABOVE: Russian troops prepare to quit their trenches and abandon the war – thereby illustrating Lenin's comment that the deserting soldiers voted for the revolution with their feet.

LEFT: A Bolshevik rally denouncing the Provisional Government's policy of continuing the war.

RIGHT: Frontline soldiers cheer the news of the outbreak of the February Revolution.

it. On a practical note, the Allies hoped that the new government would be able to wage a more efficient war.

The attitude of the Central Powers to the March Revolution was mixed: their instinctive fear of popular revolution, regarded as highly contagious, was offset by the possibility of a negotiated peace with the Provisional Government, or at least the further reduction of Russia's fighting power through internal discord. To this end the Russian revolutionary leader Vladimir Ilyich Ulyanov – Lenin – was allowed to return to Russia from exile in Switzerland.

Despite growing disaffection within the Russian Army the Minister of War, Alexander Kerensky, determined upon renewed offensive action to rekindle Russian patriotism. He had, however, overestimated the military potential of the Russian Army and failed to comprehend the growing political consciousness of the ordinary soldiers. The left-wing Soviet (council) of Workers and Soldiers' Representatives had made great inroads into the Army and in most units officers shared the powers of leadership with a politically appointed representative (or commissar, as they were later known). Almost inevitably, military efficiency declined even further.

Nevertheless a striking force of 200,000 men was assembled for an assault on the mainly Austrian positions in Galicia. On 1 July 1917 what became known as the Kerensky Offensive got underway. Some progress was made during the first week of fighting but a crushing counterblow brought the Russian advance to a dead halt. The Russian soldiers had had enough and now retreated in vast numbers. In Lenin's words, 'they voted for peace with their legs.' From August onward the Russian Army disintegrated, mutinies and mass desertions were commonplace. In September the Germans followed up their repulse of Kerensky's attack with a limited offensive of their own which saw the capture of the Baltic port of Riga by General Oscar von Hutier's Eighth Army. The attack was notable for the first use of 'predicted shooting' devised by Colonel Georg Bruchmüller. This technique restored the long-lost element of surprise, permitting a German advance of nearly 10 miles on the first day.

The weakness of the Russian Provisional Government enabled the Bolshevik faction of the Social Democrats to seize power in November 1917 (the famous 'October Revolution,' so-called because the Russian Julian calendar was 13 days behind the international system). Under the determined leadership of Lenin and Leon Trotsky, the

ABOVE LEFT: Russian troops flee from the battlefield. For over three years the Russian Army had patiently borne exceptionally heavy casualties, poor leadership and a series of morale-sapping defeats. By the summer of 1917 it had suffered enough and the revolution in February raised expectations of a peace settlement.

ABOVE: Alexander Kerensky, photographed in his cabinet rooms shortly after the formation of the Provisional Government.

LEFT: The 1917 summer offensive followed the pattern of previous attacks on the Germans in that there were large numbers of Russian prisoners to be sent to the rear.

LEFT: General Oscar von Hutier, an innovative commander who scored considerable success at the Battle of Riga by employing 'predictive shooting' to confuse the enemy.

ABOVE RIGHT: Russian troops throw down their arms, a common sight in 1917.

RIGHT: A public meeting held in Moscow to debate the merits of the Kerensky Offensive.

Bolsheviks had little trouble ousting the government. Bolshevik promises of 'Peace, Land and Bread' impressed the masses who were increasingly disillusioned with the disorganized Provisional Government which was still calling for the continuance of war from a people who had sacrificed themselves for little gain.

War or peace was the key issue in 1917 Russia and the Bolshevik Party had the people's support. In the battle for the control of Petrograd, the capital, the Bolsheviks seized the city's key positions, experiencing little opposition, before surrounding the seat of government – The Winter Palace. The armed forces had fallen apart so much that they now existed as separate units with their own particular allegiances. The Provisional Government in November 1917 could only count on a few officer cadets and a women's battalion. The Bolshevik-controlled cruiser *Aurora* moved up the Neva River and, by firing a few shells into the palace, began the Bolshevik assault. There were few casualties as both the Provisional Government and its defenders had largely melted away. The Bolsheviks marched into the Winter Palace and formed their own government. Almost immediately they began peace negotiations. The German High Command saw in this a marvelous opportunity, first to seize large areas of Russia, and secondly, to transfer the bulk of the German Army in the East to the Western Front. On 15 December 1917 an armistice agreement was signed at Brest-Litovsk, followed by peace negotiations in the New Year.

As negotiations between the German and Bolshevik representatives began, German forces moved deep into the Ukraine (whose newly formed government owed its existence to German 'patronage'), and despite the armistice invaded Russian territory from the Baltic to the Black Sea. The Bolsheviks had no means with which to oppose the Central Powers and the victors' terms for a peace settlement were harsh in the extreme. Faced with civil war and ruthless invasion, the Bolsheviks were forced to accept and the Treaty of Brest-Litovsk was signed on 3 March

1918. Russia lost 34 percent of its population and some of its most productive areas containing 54 percent of her basic industry.

Despite the view of the German High Command that the war would be decided in the West, new opportunities for expansion in the East deflected its members from their original aim. Large numbers of German troops remained in the East and continued to advance into southern Russia. The Crimea was occupied in April 1918 – in total violation of the Brest-Litovsk Treaty – and a few weeks later the Germans secured control of Rostov and the economically important Donetz basin. In the north, German units moved into Finland, and plans were drawn up for the seizure of Petrograd and the overthrow of the Bolshevik regime. Only defeat on the Western Front shattered German dreams of expansion in the East.

TOP: Red Guards defend the steps of the Smolny Institute, one of Bolsheviks' strongholds during the October Revolution.

ABOVE: V I Lenin, the Bolshevik leader and the man most atuned to the political developments of Russia in 1917.

ABOVE: The Foreign
Ministers of the Central
Powers. From the left:
Count Czernin (Austria) and
Kuhlmann (Germany). They
went to Brest-Litovsk to
impose a harsh peace
knowing that they had the
backup of the all-powerful
German Army if
negotiations broke down.

ABOVE RIGHT: The revolution
encouraged the expression
of nationalist feelings
among Russia's minority
groups. Although many of
such groups veered to the
political right, these Poles
and Lithuanians
demonstrate their support
for the Bolshevik
movement.

RIGHT: The Germans swiftly
disregarded the terms of
Brest-Litovsk and invaded
the Ukraine in 1918. Here,
German troops parade in
the center of the Ukrainian
capital of Kiev.

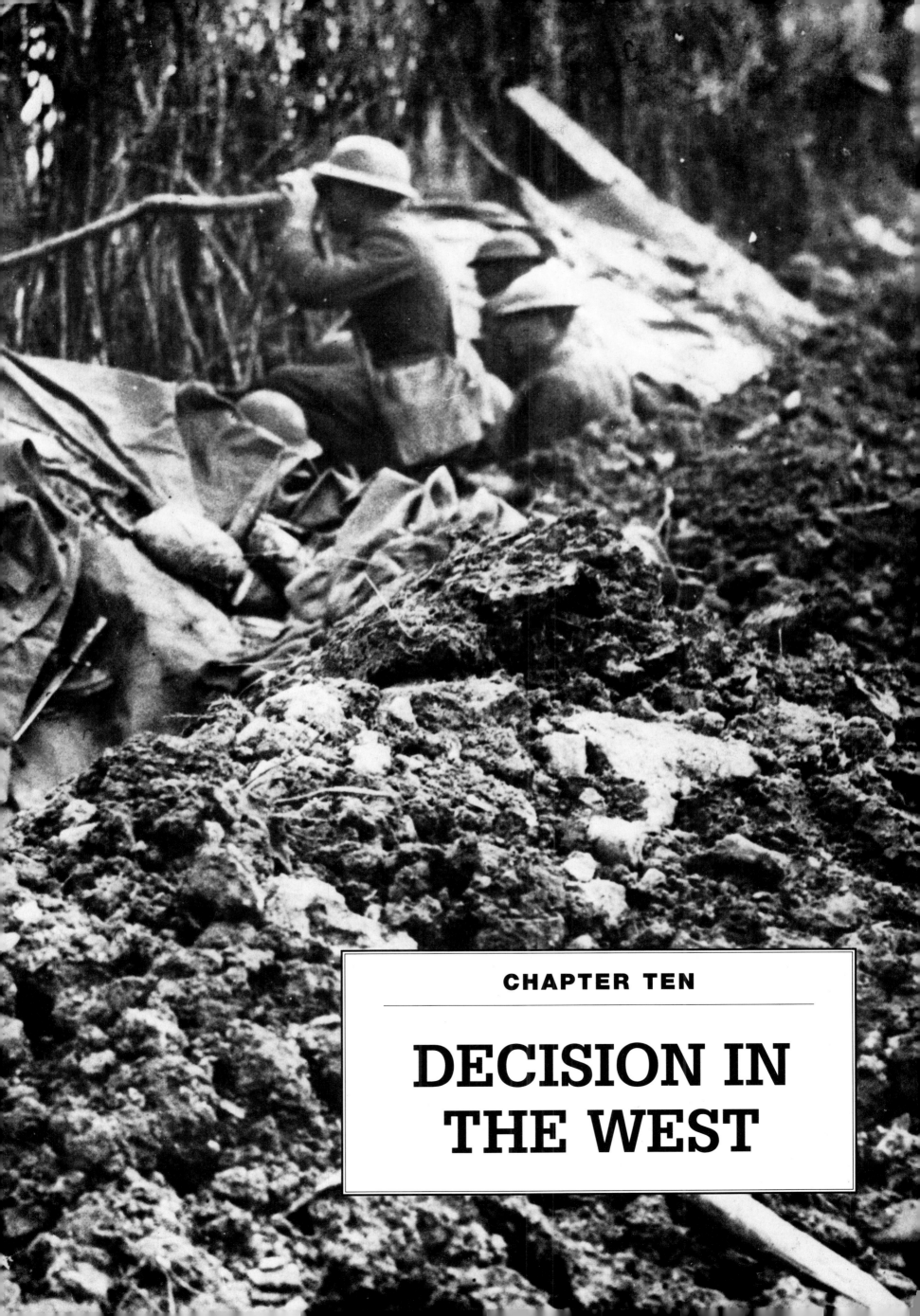

CHAPTER TEN

DECISION IN THE WEST

By the beginning of 1918 all the Allied armies were suffering from serious manpower shortages. French reserves were exhausted and it was only with considerable difficulty that 90 divisions were maintained on the Western Front. Italy was still reeling from the Caporetto disaster. Five British divisions (over 100,000 men) had been sent to the Italian front while, at the same time, strong forces were preparing a new offensive against the Turks in Palestine. Meanwhile, the government had decreed a reorganization of the BEF which meant a reduction of 141 battalions, although its front was simultaneously extended by some 25 miles.

Germany was now virtually ruled by Hindenburg and Ludendorff. They recognized that, despite the obvious weaknesses of the Allies, Germany's military position was far from secure. The heavy fighting of 1917 had gravely weakened the Army and lowered its efficiency and morale. The U-boat campaign which had been expected to decide the issue after a few months had clearly failed to do so. Germany was now suffering badly from the rigors of blockade. And although few American troops were yet in the battle line, their numbers were steadily rising and would evidently offset the German forces being released from the Eastern Front. It was a position that could only worsen, and the High Command now decided on a gambler's throw aimed at defeating the Allies outright: a spring offensive against the British armies on the Somme-Arras front.

The German High Command's decision to risk everything on a last desperate offensive was typical of the all-or-nothing approach of Ludendorff and Hindenburg. In all probability they would have done better to have maintained a defensive strategy in the West until some form of negotiated settlement could be made with the Allies. A few German politicians – including Prince Max of Baden – had tried to persuade Ludendorff to accept such a plan which would renounce any claims upon Belgian independence, thereby removing Britain's *casus belli*. But Ludendorff and most of his fellow commanders hankered after complete military victory and so the planning for the last great offensive went ahead.

German strength on the Western Front rose steadily during the early months of 1918, but the High Command did not rely solely on numbers. Throughout 1917 the Germans had developed their infiltration tactics, forming units of specialized 'stormtroopers' to carry them out. In the winter months prior to the great offensive, selected divisions were withdrawn from the line to go on special courses of instruction in these new tactical methods. By

PREVIOUS PAGES: Troops of the US Army guard a freshly captured German trench during fighting in the Meuse Valley north of Verdun, 3 October 1918.

TOP: The de facto rulers of Germany in 1918, Hindenburg (left) and Ludendorff. Their authority extended over almost all forms of industrial and commercial activity.

ABOVE: Training for the great day of breakthrough on the Western Front, German stormtroopers manhandle a trench mortar.

LEFT: A German machine-gun unit prepares to set up a gun in open fields near Ypres during the Lys offensive of April 1918.

ABOVE: *A German 21cm howitzer is slowly hauled toward its emplacement in preparation for Bruchmüller's carefully orchestrated fire plan.*

BELOW: *21 March 1918 – German infantry dash forward over No Man's Land with the utmost rapidity in order to overwhelm the battered British troops holding a badly damaged trench line.*

BELOW RIGHT: *A long-range heavy field gun is used to fire upon British positions.*

the end of 1917 it was apparent to any battlefield commander that promising advances would often become bogged down due to the activities of small groups of defenders holed up in strong positions. Infiltration tactics meant that the attackers, moving in small well-armed groups, could by-pass these strongpoints, leaving them to be dealt with by later waves of attackers specially equipped and armed to overcome these defenses. The attackers would always try to press on, keeping the momentum of the offensive going, and by positioning themselves behind the defenders, could cause them maximum confusion. These tactics called for high-quality infantrymen, brave, resourceful and capable of using their own initiative when separated from their officers and senior NCOs. Consequently, the 'storm' divisions became the German Army's elite. They were provided with better

arms and equipment and a larger ration allowance, as well as generally being excused trench-holding duties. At the same time, of course, this policy tended to reduce the fighting capabilities of the ordinary divisions, especially as they lost some of their best men to the 'storm troops.' The new tactics were first introduced toward the end of 1917: during the Caporetto offensive of October and in the counterattack at Cambrai on 30 November. Their success was striking.

In addition the massive German artillery concentration planned to use the technique of predicted shooting which had been so successful at Riga; once again orchestrated by Bruchmüller. During February and March 1918 preparations were made for the coming offensive. German staffwork was excellent: guns, ammunition, supplies and men were brought forward with utmost secrecy.

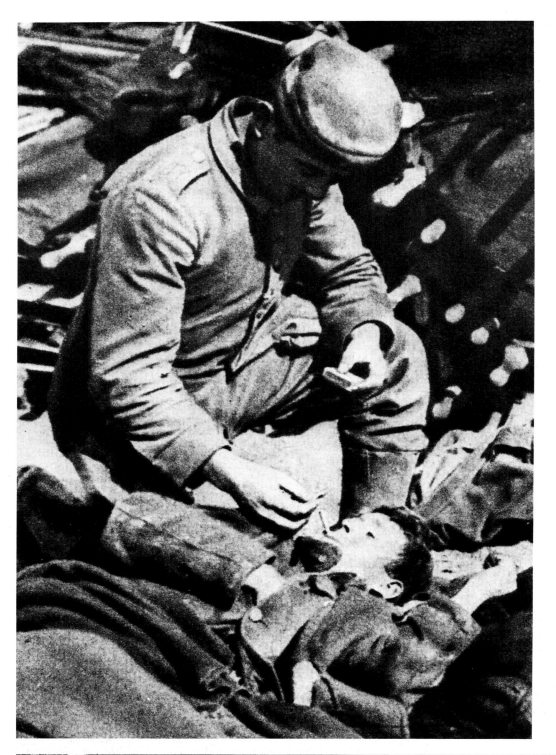

Codenamed Operation Michael, the German offensive was carried out by the Seventeenth Army (Below), the Second Army (von der Marwitz) and the Eighteenth Army (Hutier). A total of 59 divisions were earmarked for the offensive. The assault was supported by the largest concentration of artillery ever assembled: 6473 guns and howitzers and 3532 trench mortars. Along a front of 50 miles the Germans were faced with the 12 infantry divisions of the British Fifth Army (Gough) and, further to the north, General Byng's Third Army of 14 divisions. The Fifth Army had just taken over a section of the French line and had still not completed its defenses when Operation Michael was launched. The staff of the Fifth Army had accurately predicted the German attack, but Gough's army was weak in relation to the length of front held and there were very few reserves behind it.

As the units of the Fifth Army took over their incomplete positions – parts of the reserve line consisted of tape indicating where the trenches should be dug – they were further hampered by a new tactical policy adopted by the British Army. Previously the British had relied on a linear approach to defensive tactics with large numbers of men deployed in forward trenches for the immediate repulse of the enemy. The new system of 'elastic defense' was neither fully understood nor popular among the Fifth Army, and resources were insufficient for the plan to be properly implemented. The 'elastic defense' consisted of a lightly held forward line which was intended to merely hold up the enemy advance while the main action was fought out within the battle zone, directly behind the forward line. Influenced by the success of German defensive methods during the 1917 battles, the new British system advocated the construction of mutually supportive strongholds as opposed to the even defense of linear trench systems. In March 1917, however, these strongpoints were incomplete and rarely mutually supportive, resulting in many cases of dangerous isolation.

The massed German guns opened the great offensive with a shattering five-hour bombardment at 0510 hours on 21 March 1918. Bruchmüller's artillery plan went according to schedule: the long-range guns fired on railroad junctions far to the rear, preventing the movement of reinforcements; British gun positions were hammered by gas and high-explosive attacks; the main trench positions received continuous bombardment, virtually obliterating the hastily dug British defenses; and the numerous trench

ABOVE LEFT: A captured British casualty receives a cigarette from a German medical orderly during the early stages of the Michael Offensive.

LEFT: A second wave of German troops advances through the barricaded streets of Bailleul. The swiftness of the German advance during the first few days of the offensive seemed to presage an outright breakthrough.

mortars were employed to destroy the wire and forward outposts. A thick morning mist proved invaluable to the attacking storm troops, and the badly battered British frontline positions were overrun with comparative ease. By the end of the first day's fighting both the Fifth and Third Armies were in retreat. British casualties on 21 March were estimated at 38,512 (including 21,000 prisoners), but the Germans had suffered even greater losses. During the next week the British continued to retreat as Ludendorff exploited his initial success. By the end of March, 83 German divisions had been engaged in the battle.

As the German advance continued, a grave risk of separation faced the Allied armies. General Pétain feared a further attack on the French sector and was reluctant to support the British. To overcome this and at Haig's instigation, a unified command was set up on 26 March. General Ferdinand Foch was appointed to co-ordinate all British and French forces. French units were then moved northward to aid the hard-pressed British.

ABOVE RIGHT: A battery of German artillery fires at British positions from the relative safety of a wood.

RIGHT: Although Pétain feared a major attack on his own sector he eventually sent reinforcements to the hard-pressed British. Here, French and British troops dig new trenches to cover a road in the Somme region, 25 March 1918.

BELOW: Men of the 12th East Yorks look across No Man's Land from their trenches around Arieux. Box periscopes are employed to protect observers from the attentions of German snipers.

Operation Michael: 21 March 1918

Operation Michael was the German High Command's great gamble, the last chance to resolve the trench deadlock of the Western Front by an outright military victory. The first phase of the battle – the breakthrough – was to depend largely on Colonel Bruchmüller's artillery plan. This consisted of a whirlwind bombardment intended to last only five hours and divided into seven separate phases with various classes of gun moving from target to target in accordance with each changing phase. Altogether 6473 guns and 3532 trench mortars were secretly assembled and hidden along the front line. At 0440 hours the bombardment began, an awesome experience for the watching Germans and 'all hell let loose' for the British. Second Lieutenant H V Crees, 22nd Northumberland Fusiliers, was an actual witness to the opening seconds of Bruchmüller's artillery attack:

I was going round inspecting the posts and just happened to be standing on the firestep with my head just over the parapet, looking out over No Man's Land. Then I saw this colossal flash of light. As far as I could see, from left to right, was lit up by it. I heard nothing for a few seconds and, for a moment, I wondered what it was. I think I just managed to hear the gunfire itself before the shells arrived all around us.

LEFT: *Exhausted German troops rest alongside a column of motorized transport in the newly captured town of Albert.*

BELOW: *Men of the New Zealand Division, march by Whippet tanks to plug a gap in the line, 26 March 1918. The higher top speed, greater maneuverability and reliability of the Whippets over the standard British tanks suggested a great future for this new weapon of war.*

BELOW: The 'blind leading the blind' – gas casualties await treatment at an Advanced Dressing Station near Béthune, 10 April 1918.

BOTTOM: John Singer Sargent's Gassed *owed its inspiration to the scenes depicted in the photograph above.*

By 28 March, having penetrated the British lines to a maximum depth of 40 miles, the German effort began to weaken. Although both the Germans and British had been surprised at the completeness of the Fifth Army's collapse on 21 March, the British generally retreated in good order, forcing the Germans to fight their way forward. The Germans, for their part, had suffered heavy casualties, and as the German troops began to overrun British supply dumps, widespread looting set in. The poorly provisioned German soldiers were dismayed by the amount and quality of food available to the British. Many German soldiers refused their officers' orders in favor of looting – the first signs of growing ill-discipline which would reach dangerous proportions in the coming

months. Also, the German Army had few cavalry on the Western Front and so there was no possibility for the Germans to exploit the breakthrough. In addition, the forward troops were beginning to run short of ammunition and were forced to wait for horse-drawn transport wagons to make their way across the battlefield with further supplies.

The British Third Army repulsed an assault against Arras, while the key center of Amiens remained just out of German reach. Having failed to break the British with the Michael Offensive, a second blow (Operation George, later reduced to 'Georgette') was delivered further north in Flanders along the River Lys on 9 April. Again, the German attack was preceded by a massive bombardment and

ABOVE LEFT: A French armored car acts in support of British troops at Materen during the Battle of the Lys, 14 April 1918.

ABOVE: One of the more exotic implements of trench warfare, a canvas and steel 'tree' observation post, seen here from the back. Both Germans and British employed these 'trees' in exposed positions.

LEFT: A scene from the Third Battle of the Aisne, May 1918 – a British band rests by the roadside while a unit of veteran French infantry moves forward. This battle marked the high point of the German advances in 1918.

ABOVE RIGHT: A German corpse lies face downward on the side of Mount Kemmel, a victim of the Lys attacks in April 1918.

RIGHT: German stormtroopers advance over the Chemin des Dames to reinforce their compatriots fighting on the old Aisne battlefield.

initial progress was good. Shortages of British reserves – which were stemming the German flood on the Somme to the south – rendered the situation extremely grim and the British troops were forced to hang on without support. On 11 April the normally reticent Haig felt forced to issue his famous statement: 'Every position must be held to the last man. There must be no retirement. With our backs to the wall and believing in the justice of our cause each one must fight on to the end. The safety of our homes and the freedom of mankind alike depend upon the conduct of each one of us at this critical moment.'

The German pressure continued throughout the month but the Allied line held, and the results were even more disappointing than those encountered in the Michael Offensive. Flanders nevertheless continued to be Ludendorff's favored theater of operations. He realized, however, that before he attacked the British again he first had to force the withdrawal of the French divisions (13 infantry and three cavalry) from the British sector. Accordingly, a heavy diversionary attack was planned on the *Chemin des Dames* in Champagne. Great secrecy surrounded the German preparations, which included the assembly of 4000 guns on a narrow front, once more under the direction of Bruchmüller. The attack, known as the Third Battle of the Aisne, began at 0100 hours on 27 May and took the French command entirely by surprise. Its success surprised even the Germans: the first day saw the deepest single-day penetration on the Western Front of the whole war. By 3 June the Germans had once again reached the River Marne.

The German line, now forming a huge bulge, invited a counterattack. Their attempts to broaden it met with little success and the French, reinforced by British, American and even Italian divisions, prepared a counterstroke. The last German offensive of the war was launched on 15 June

LEFT: *A trench scene by the British artist Paul Nash entitled* The Ypres Salient at Night. *British troops man a trench in the foreground while the night sky is lit up by star-shell explosions.*

RIGHT: *An illustration of American artillery forcing their guns through a French village. The US Army began to make an important contribution to the Allied cause on the Western Front during the latter stages of the German Aisne-Second Marne onslaught.*

BELOW: *A distinctive painting by the British artist C R W Nevinson depicting a group of French soldiers resting by the roadside.*

BELOW RIGHT: *An American 'doughboy' in action in the streets of Chateau Thierry.*

Battle for Belleau Wood

The US Marines have always claimed a special place in the American armed forces as the toughest infantry fighters. Their US Army 'rivals' had made their mark on 1 June 1918 when the 1st Division had conducted a brilliant attack against the Germans at Cantigny. Not to be outdone, the Marines were determined to outshine this feat; their chance came a few days later during their counterattack against the last stages of the German advance through the tangled mass of Belleau Wood:

> Across this wheatfield there were more woods, and in the edge of these woods the old Boche, lots of them, infantry and machine guns. Surely he had seen the platoons forming a few hundred yards away – it is possible that he did not believe his eyes. He let them come close before he opened fire. The American fighting man has his failings. He is prone to many regrettable errors. But the sagacious enemy will never let him get close enough to see whom he is attacking. When he has seen the enemy, the American regular will come on in. To stop him you must kill him. And when he is properly trained and has somebody to say 'Come on!' to him, he will stand as much killing as anybody on earth.
>
> The platoons, assailed now by a fury of smallarms fire, narrowed their eyes and inclined their bodies forward, like men in heavy rain, and went on. Second waves reinforced the first, fourth waves the third, as prescribed. Officers yelled 'Battlesight! Fire at will' – and the leaders, making out green-gray, clumsy uniforms and round pot-helmets in the gloom of the woods, took it up with Springfields, aimed shots. Automatic riflemen brought their 'chaut-chauts' into action from the hip – a 'chaut-chaut' is as accurate from the hip as it ever is – and wrangled furiously with their supporting ammunition-carriers.
>
> A spray of fugitive Boche went before the attack, holding where the ground offered cover, working his light machine gun with devilish skill, retiring, on the whole, commendably. He had not expected to fight a defensive battle here, and was not heavily entrenched, but the place was stiff with his troops and he was in good quality, as Marine casualty lists were presently to show.
>
> Men crawled forward; the wheat was agitated and the Boche, directing his fire by observers in treetops, browned the slope industriously. Men were wounded, wounded again as the lines of fire swept back and forth, and finally killed. It helped some to bag the feld-webels in the trees; there were men in that line who could hit at 750 yards three times out of five. Sweating, hot, and angry with a bleak, cold anger, the Marines worked forward. They were there and the Germans, and there was nothing else in the clanging world. A man can stand just so much of that. Life presently ceases to be desirable; the only desirable thing is to kill that gunner, kill him with your hands! One of them, a corporal named Geer, said: 'By God, let's get him!' And they got him. One fellow seized the spitting muzzle and up-ended it on the gunner; he lost a hand in the matter. Bayonets flashed in, and a rifle-butt rose and fell. The battle tore through the coppice. The machine-gunners were brave men and many of the Prussian infantry were brave men, and they died.

CAPTAIN JOHN W THOMASON,
5th US Marines.

ABOVE: Marshal Ferdinand Foch, victor of the Second Battle of the Marne and generalissimo of the Allied armies on the Western Front.

BELOW LEFT: Wearing gas masks a Lewis machine-gun team fends off a German attack, June 1918.

ABOVE RIGHT: German A7V tanks go into action on the Western Front near Villers-Brettoneaux. The only tank manufactured by the Germans, the A7V was too big and cumbersome to be truly effective, and compared poorly with British models.

RIGHT: A group of French troops who were fatally caught by a heavy German bombardment of a sunken road near Courcelles, June 1918.

but immediately ground to a halt. On 18 June Foch hit back – the Second Battle of the Marne – a victory which marked the passing of the strategic initiative on the Western Front to the Allies at last.

More immediately, it marked the end of any possibility of another German attack on the British in Flanders. Instead the BEF prepared for a new offensive which began on 8 August, a date which Ludendorff called 'the black day of the German Army.' On that day the Australians, Canadians and British troops of General Rawlinson's Fourth Army, with a French army attacking beside them, opened the Battle of Amiens. As at Cambrai in 1917, the initial success was obtained by a devastating bombardment of predicted shooting, followed by the onset of 414 fighting tanks masked by a dense fog. The Canadians and Australians smashed through the German lines and only the British III Corps, on the far left of the line, experienced any real difficulties. By the end of the first day's fighting, the Fourth Army had penetrated the German defenses up to a distance of eight miles, killed and wounded 13,000 enemy soldiers, taken 15,000 prisoners and 400 guns, for a loss of 17,000 of their own men.

The importance of the victory at Amiens lay in the effect it had on German morale. For the first time since the war

LEFT: *An early example of 'self-propelled' artillery, a British gun-carrier tank transports a 6-inch howitzer (and its ammunition) to a firing emplacement.*

RIGHT: *A German soldier has an arm wound dressed up by a medical orderly.*

BELOW: *Updated Mark V tanks of the 4th Battalion drive through the key town of Meaulte, consolidating British advances.*

BELOW RIGHT: *In preparation for the crossing of the St Quentin Canal, tanks with 'cribs' are brought up to the front line with the utmost secrecy. 'Cribs' were used to fill in ditches or similar tank obstacles to overcome the early tanks' problems with mobility.*

Air-Ground Operations 1918

At the outset of the war in August 1914, military aviation was concerned with extending the cavalry's function of reconnaissance, but as the war continued, aircraft began to find new roles, to the extent that by 1918 the importance of British aviation was such that it had gained independent status as the Royal Air Force, alongside the Navy and the Army. Long-range strategic bombing was only on the horizon in 1918 so the most useful tasks undertaken by military aviation were those in direct support of ground troops. Reconnaissance duties had developed into the regular photographic mapping of German lines, while the artillery benefited from the provision of precise and immediate details of the accuracy of their guns, making 'firing-over-the-hill' a feasible operation.

Although the aircraft had been greatly improved during the war, communications between the pilot in the air and the troops on the ground remained a fundamental problem; wireless telegraphy was the standard means of transmitting messages from air to ground, but the system was necessarily primitive. Despite this continuing weak link, co-operation between air and ground troops had made good progress within the British armed forces by the last great battles in the summer and autumn of 1918.

One of the recurring problems in any World War I offensive was that of resupply from the rear across a shell-blasted No Man's Land to the forward troops; on numerous occasions attacks ground to a halt through lack of supplies and ammunition. Aircraft were a partial solution, and by 1918 a number of successful airdrops had been made. At Le Hamel on 4 July, for example, Australian machine-gunners received 100,000 rounds of ammunition dropped from the air, while during the 'Last' Battle of Ypres in early October 1918, Allied troops were supplied with 15,000 rations from the air. Some 80 air-craft were involved in the latter operation, dropping sacks filled with five to 10 rations each packed in a 'cushion' of earth and dropped from a height of 300 feet.

Aircraft were also engaged in the art of concealment. On a number of occasions – the Battle of Amiens was one – low-flying aircraft obscured the noise of tanks moving up to the front line prior to an attack. Phosphorus bombs were employed to produce rudimentary smoke screens, and during the advance near Serain on 8 October 1918, the deployment of XIII Corps was concealed by an aircraft-manufactured smoke screen which was maintained for two hours over the Allied front.

For such coordination between ground and air to succeed, however, liaison officers from both the Army and Air Force had to win each other's confidence. Thus, for example, during the last months of the war the Tank Corps developed a fruitful relationship with RAF squadrons working alongside them. A standard practice was for a tank officer to fly in the observer's cockpit to gain an aerial overview of the battlefield, while the 'displaced' observer would go forward with the tanks in order to understand the special problems encountered by the tank crews.

The RAF was not merely concerned with simple co-operation techniques. It carried out its own offensive operation in support of the ground forces. The Germans pioneered ground-attack operations during the Cambrai counteroffensive in November 1917, and for the spring offensive in 1918 specially designed aircraft were deployed to strafe ground troops with machine guns and bombs. The British quickly followed the German lead, so that large numbers of well-armored and armed aircraft dominated the battlefields of the summer and fall of 1918, shooting up enemy entrenchments, transports, other road vehicles and any other suitable targets.

began whole German divisions had fallen back without a fight, while thousands of men had been captured with little or no resistance. And when reinforcements were rushed forward to plug the gap, they were met with abuse from the retiring troops, who called them 'blacklegs' and 'warmongerers.' The decline in morale was felt even at the top, causing Ludendorff to write: 'Our war machine is no longer efficient. Our fighting power has suffered and 8 August put the decline of that fighting power beyond all doubt.' On 11 August the Kaiser and the top German generals held a conference at Avesnes, after which the Kaiser was forced to conclude: 'I see that we must strike a balance. We have nearly reached the limit of our power of resistance. The war must be ended.' German diplomats were instructed to make definitive soundings for a negotiated peace.

Rawlinson's army was now approaching the shattered landscape of the 1916 Somme battlefields, a formidable obstacle. Haig was determined not to become bogged down in this ill-omened area and now steadily extended his front of attack northward, bringing in the Third Army (Byng) on 21 August (the Battle of Albert) and the First

Army (Horne) on 26 August (the Battle of the Scarpe). The British advance was continuous; on their right the French attacked at Noyon, and on 12 September the Americans fought and won their first great battle at St Mihiel. Here two US corps caught the Germans withdrawing from the St Mihiel salient and inflicted heavy casualties on them. The Americans had given notice to the world that they were a force to be reckoned with.

The climax of the whole Allied offensive came in late September with the British attack on the Hindenburg Line, while the French and Americans opened a new offensive in the Argonne. The American Expeditionary Force had to be transferred northward from St Mihiel to their start position for the Argonne offensive with the

Breakdown of an Army

This account taken from a German soldier's diary during the last months of the war reveals the many cracks which were appearing in the once mighty edifice of the Imperial German Army:

Imagine a series of stinking rooms which yesterday or the day before were a chateau. The wind and rain come in at the windows, in which fragments of glass tinkle at every shellburst. The walls tremble all day and all night. When the heavy shells are seeking out their mark by degrees and draw nearer, the men run to the cellar . . . Stretcher-cases get smothered there in the darkness of the night by others who are trying to get shelter. The place stinks of blood, sweat, urine, excrement, iodoform and wet clothes. Down below in the passages they peel potatoes, and nobody thinks of throwing away the peel; one puts down the wounded on top of it. The house rings day and night with cries of pain, but with craven and selfish demands as well. The numbers of dead on the lawn of the park steadily increase, while the scum of the army stand around and stare at them with revolting curiosity. In the corner there is a man digging graves without ceasing.

utmost rapidity, a maneuver which proved too much for the American staff organization. Once the battle got underway the US forces showed a forceful resolution in attacking the German positions, but their advance slowed due to logistic shortcomings. Nonetheless they refused to give up the attack which continued for 47 days of almost continuous fighting. Once supplies to the forward troops were put on a sound footing (with the help of French and British staff officers) the Americans steadily pushed the Germans back.

A mixed Belgian-British-French army group attacked in Flanders. On 29 September the British Fourth Army broke through the Hindenburg Line – a magnificent feat of arms which produced 35,000 prisoners and 380 captured guns. The crossing of the St Quentin Canal at Bellenglise by the 46th (South Midland) Division was particularly spectacular: the steep-sided canal was crossed in the face of heavy machine-gun and artillery fire. By the end of the day the troops had captured 4200 prisoners for the loss of only 800 men. This was the beginning of the end. It was on this day that the German High Command concluded that the only thing to do was to make an immediate approach to US President Woodrow Wilson requesting his good offices for an armistice and peace.

LEFT: *The assault on the Hindenburg Line – British tanks and infantry guard battlefield prisoners on captured ground near Bellicourt, 29 September 1918.*

BELOW LEFT: *A few of the many German prisoners captured during the final months of war.*

RIGHT: *French-built Renault light tanks of the US Army press forward in pursuit of the retiring Germans.*

BELOW: *Troops of the 23rd Infantry Division move forward under fire during the reduction of the St Mihiel salient by the US First Army.*

CHAPTER ELEVEN

DEFEAT OF THE CENTRAL POWERS

From the very beginning Germany's allies were as much a liability as an asset. All leaned heavily on German weaponry and munitions, on German expertise and on German forces fighting on their various fronts. Their value to Germany lay in their diversionary capability and this turned out to be a considerable advantage: the Austro-Hungarians against Russia, the Turks against Britain and the Bulgarians against the large Allied force locked up in Salonika. As the war continued, however, all three grew steadily weaker and more dependent on outside aid which became more and more difficult to supply as Germany's own position deteriorated.

Turkey, having been almost continuously at war since 1911 and ruling over a largely disaffected Arab population, was perhaps the weakest of all. Her last attempt to reach the Suez Canal, in July 1916, was easily repelled. By the end of that year the British forces from Egypt under General Sir Archibald Murray had reached the border of Palestine (building a railway and laying a water pipeline as they went). An attempt to advance farther in March 1917 was checked at Gaza by a combination of British error and the stubborn defensive quality of the Turkish soldiers – a quality already demonstrated at Gallipoli. Murray was recalled in June 1917 and replaced by General Sir Edmund Allenby. Alongside Haig and Gough, Allenby was a cavalry general who, like them, found his grand schemes for battles of maneuver frustrated on the Western Front. Allenby's appointment to Palestine at last gave him a chance to fight the sort of war he had been trained for, and he was particularly fortunate in having at his disposal a large number of cavalry units including substantial contingents from Australia, New Zealand and India.

The British Prime Minister made it clear to Allenby that he expected dramatic military success. In a year of military disappointments, Lloyd George was determined that Jerusalem would fall to British forces by the end of the year – what he called his 'Christmas present to the British nation.' Allenby was accordingly given powerful reinforcements which had been withheld from Murray.

Allenby spent the summer months preparing his forces

for the coming offensive. The Turkish positions around Gaza were well developed and the Turks were formidable defensive fighters. Consequently Allenby planned to smash his way through the Turkish defenses further inland, capture the town of Beersheba and finally turn and take Gaza from the rear. Ingenious (and successful) plans were instigated to deceive the Turks into believing the attack would in fact be launched directly against Gaza. Turkish forces in Palestine were under the command of the peripatetic General Erich von Falkenhayn, and were undergoing a general reorganization after the release of troops from the Russian theater of operations following the 1917 Revolution.

Allenby made his move on 31 October and achieved a significant numerical superiority over the Turks, particularly in cavalry – a ratio of 10 to one. Beersheba fell to a cavalry attack delivered by an Australian mounted brigade which swept through the village with bayonets drawn – there was a temporary shortage of swords. The British forces then wheeled westward toward Gaza and the coast, and after a fierce battle which included a bombardment of the town by British warships, the Turks abandoned Gaza on 7 November and fell back northward. Although they had lost 10,000 prisoners, the Turkish retreat was made in good order and the British cavalry's brave and forceful attempt to cut off the main Turkish force was unsuccessful.

The onset of the rainy season, expected at any moment, encouraged Allenby to press on with the utmost speed. Before Falkenhayn could mount an effective counterattack, the British had advanced along the coast to Jaffa and into the Judean hills, forcing the Turks to fall back from Jerusalem. On 11 December the British took possession of the Holy City and, as a public gesture of Christian humility, Allenby and his staff walked through the gates to accept the surrender. Allenby had given Lloyd George his 'Christmas present.' Jerusalem had no strategic importance but to the Christian world it was of obvious religious significance as Western propagandists were quick to emphasise. In an otherwise disappointing year for the

PREVIOUS PAGES: The end of the old Ottoman Empire – Turkish troops, captured after the action at Tuz Khurmath, are searched by men of the 38th Lancashire Brigade, 29 April 1918.

RIGHT: Building on their experience of utilizing available animal power in the colonies, the British built up the Imperial Camel Corps for deployment in Palestine.

BELOW LEFT: Troopers of the 14th (Kings) Hussars rest on their return from an action against the Turks at Jebel Hamrin, December 1917.

BELOW RIGHT: Allenby's capture of Jerusalem in December 1917 brought the British some much-needed cheer in an otherwise generally unsuccessful year. Here, Allenby takes the salute of local boy scouts.

BELOW, FAR RIGHT: The German commander of the Central Powers' forces in Palestine, General Falkenhayn (second left), confers with Turkish officers.

Allies, it was a tangible success and augured well for the future of the war.

While Allenby's conventional forces pressed northward along the Palestinian coast, farther inland the Turks were harried by a guerrilla force of Arab tribesmen under the leadership of Emir Feisal and a British liaison officer, Colonel T E Lawrence. To the tribesmen, Lawrence was 'El Uruns,' a legendary figure who, with Feisal, offered the Arabs a vision of national unity through victory over the Turks. An archaeologist and Arabist before the outbreak of war, Lawrence was posted to Cairo as an intelligence officer. When in June 1916 the Arabs of the Hejaz rose up against the Turks Lawrence was despatched to Arabia to report on the revolt. Once there, however, he extended the scope of his brief to collaborate with Feisal in transforming a simple revolt into a full-scale guerrilla war. The first phase of the campaign lasted from June 1916 to July 1917 and consisted of guerrilla raids against the Hejaz railway running south from Palestine to Medina. Lawrence's policy was not to destroy the railway outright but to impede its running, thereby drawing large numbers of Turkish troops from other theaters of war to guard the line. In the middle of 1917 the Arab guerrillas stepped up the campaign and in July they mounted a daring raid on the port of Aqaba which fell on the 6th.

The second phase of the campaign now began as the Arab guerrillas moved northward out of Arabia to operate on the desert flank of the main British forces in Palestine. The British supplied the Arabs with armaments, eventually including light artillery and armored cars. Most importantly, they also provided gold to keep the tribesmen in the field now that they were fighting far from their desert homes. Working loosely with Allenby the guerrillas helped guard the open British right flank while generally harrying Turkish lines of communication.

Relations between the Arabs and the British were to become increasingly strained, however, as the former realized that the idea of an Arab state had been fatally compromised by British promises to the Jews of a national state in Palestine – the famous Balfour Declaration of 1917

ABOVE: Turkish troops rise from their trenches in an attack against British positions. Even after their defeat at Gaza, the Turks were far from a broken force.

LEFT: Colonel T E Lawrence, the British intelligence officer who was sent into Arabia to assess the Arab revolt, went on to become a renowned guerrilla leader and desert legend.

RIGHT: A photograph of Emir Feisal and his hand-picked bodyguards, camel-mounted tribesmen sworn to guard their leader.

RIGHT: The camp and horse lines of the 9th Australian Light Horse in a valley near Jericho, August 1918. Australian riding skills were highly valued in Palestine.

BELOW: The aftermath of the Battle of Sharon, September 1918, which saw the capture of 1200 Turks by the Desert Mounted Corps.

– and the Sykes-Picot Agreement which allowed for an Anglo-French division of the Turkish Empire after the war. In order to assert their territorial claims Feisal and the Arab champion Lawrence pushed ahead with renewed vigor and brought their campaign to a victorious conclusion with their entry into Damascus on 1 October 1918. Despite their efforts, which included representation by Lawrence at the Versailles Conference in 1919, the Arabs were poorly rewarded in the postwar settlement.

After the fall of Jerusalem the British paused to prepare for a renewed offensive when the rainy season lifted in April. Their success had been bought at a price: the disproportionate diversion of British forces from the Western Front where the Germans were about to launch their decisive stroke of March-April 1918. It became essential to call back British troops from the Middle East, thus putting a

Artillery

The most prolific types of artillery used in World War I were the relatively lightweight field guns of a caliber of around three inches (75mm) which were able to move and fight alongside the armies in the field. The swift end to mobile warfare on the Western Front reduced the effectiveness of field artillery whose flat trajectories and light warheads were unable to demolish trench defenses. As large numbers of these artillery pieces already existed, they were still used throughout the war and were found to be useful in direct support of the infantry. Also, in the more open fighting encountered on the Eastern Front and in the Middle East, they were an essential element within the artillery arm of service. The best-known types were the British 18-pounder, the German 7.7cm field gun, the Russian 76.2mm field gun and the famous French 75mm mle 1897, the first field gun of the war, which had an unequaled rate of fire of up to 28 rounds per minute.

Complementing conventional field guns were light field howitzers. These were similar in weight but fired a heavier shell with a high trajectory which made them better for bombarding trench systems. A short range of often little more than 6500 yards (against the 12,000 yards of the French '75,' for example) was an obvious limitaton to the light howitzer, but again it was its small warhead that was the essential problem. Therefore the large-caliber guns ('heavies') were the key artillery element, capable of destroying concrete emplacements and all but the deepest dugouts. The Germans led the way with heavy artillery from the long-range 15cm gun (much feared by the infantry for the speed of its shell's arrival, giving virtually no warning) to the enormous 42cm M-Gerat, better known as 'Big Bertha' which was capable of firing a 1786lb shell to a range of 10,000 yards. Austria–Hungary fielded the 308mm Skoda Model 1911 howitzer which was used to good effect on both the Western and Eastern Fronts to demolish the toughest fortification systems. Firing a heavy shell of 842lb, it had a maximum range of 10,500 yards. The French were slow to develop modern heavy artillery, but the 220mm mle 1917 Schneider was based on a long-barreled naval gun which gave it an excellent range of nearly 25,000 yards and a still effective shell weight of 231lb. The British fielded a comprehensive range of heavy howitzers, including the six-inch, eight-inch, 9.2-inch, 12-inch and 15-inch howitzers, although it was only in 1916 that the British Army began to receive adequate support from the heavies during an offensive.

Artillery tactics changed over the course of the war, although the gun remained the king of the battlefield from the beginning to the end of the conflict. At first the problems of simply organizing vast numbers of guns (and their equipment) and assessing prewar artillery doctrines against the actual experience of war took up the artillery commanders' time. The French and Germans were quick to develop new techniques, notably the creeping barrage in which a mass of guns fired along a set line which was slowly increased deeper into enemy territory and behind which the infantry advanced.

The great battles of 1915 and 1916 were invariably preceded by long artillery bombardments lasting for anything up to three weeks in the hope of pulverizing the enemy positions. As the war developed this technique was replaced by the short 'hurricane' or 'whirlwind' bombardment in which the guns were assembled with the greatest of secrecy and only a short bombardment of a few hours supported the infantry attack. Improvements in ballistics and range-finding allowed the old system of 'registration' (in which a gun would 'find' its proposed target for the offensive by firing a number of ranging shots to ensure accuracy), to be replaced by 'predicted' shooting (the target's range would be worked out on the map without firing a shot). These techniques, of course, restored the element of surprise to the battlefield and made possible the success of the German counterattack at Cambrai in 1917 and, on a greater scale, the offensive of 21 March 1918.

The British, too, scored notable artillery breakthroughs in their great offensive battles of 1918.

One other notable feature of the artillery war was the great increase in the number of guns employed during the course of the conflict. Thus, for example, the Germans had over 6000 guns available for the opening of the March offensive of 1918, whereas for the attack on Verdun they deployed only 1200 guns. On the Allied side too, the numbers of guns increased similarly, so that for a major offensive in 1918 there might be more artillerymen than infantry. World War I was indeed 'an artilleryman's war.'

60-pounder medium field guns in action, Samarra, 1918.

ABOVE LEFT: Indian cavalry ride through the streets of the newly recaptured city of Kut, 24 February 1917. Townshend's defeat was at last avenged.

ABOVE: Good transport was an important factor in the British Army's eventual success in Mesopotamia. The ability of caterpillar tractors to haul heavy loads can be appreciated from this photograph.

LEFT: A battery of artillery in action on the Mesopotamian plain. As the fall of shot from a field gun could be in excess of 10,000 yards, adequate observation was essential and the use of special observation platforms (left) was particularly valuable. As a concession to the observer's exposed position, a shield – proof against smallarms fire – was provided.

stop to offensive operations. However, the use of large numbers of Indian Army reinforcements made it possible to renew the offensive in September. The Battle of Megiddo was a complete victory for Allenby who made good use of his large contingent of cavalry as well as a small number of aircraft. The Turks were routed and their army disintegrated. The Arabs had entered Damascus on 1 October; Aleppo was captured on 26 October. In this sustained offensive and pursuit, Allenby had taken 75,000 prisoners at a cost of 5600 casualties – an indication of the utter collapse of a once-determined enemy.

Fighting in Mesopotamia took much the same course. After their surrender at Kut in April 1916, the British adopted a defensive policy and concentrated on improving their rail and river communications. Reinforcements of Indian troops were brought in and heavy artillery accumulated. All this enabled the new Commander in Chief, General Sir Stanley Maude, to begin an advance up the Tigris in December. On 24 February 1917 the British re-entered Kut and on 11 March they took Baghdad. There followed a lengthy pause during the hot season for consolidation, but Maude resumed his advance in September against a very weak enemy, one deprived of reinforcements by Allenby's threat in Palestine. On 18 November, in the middle of his skillful operations, General Maude died of cholera and was succeeded by Lieutenant General Sir William Marshall under whom the advance continued until the advent of the next hot season in March 1918.

Meanwhile, the cataclysmic events in Russia – the fall of the emperor and the start of a civil war in 1918 – gave the Mesopotamian theater a new, if modest, importance. Under Major General Dunsterville an expedition known as 'Dunsterforce' was despatched from Baghdad to co-operate with 'White' Russian troops on the Caspian Sea and to protect the oilfields around Baku from a threatened German-Turkish invasion. In September this force was withdrawn; the British campaign in Mesopotamia ended shortly afterward when the Turkish Army surrendered.

LEFT: *The forward gun of HMS* Sedgefly *is directed against a Turkish target alongside the River Tigris. These specially built flat-bottomed river boats were a great aid to the British, both as a mobile artillery spearhead and as a means of transport.*

TOP RIGHT: *British troops take over a Turkish 7.7cm field gun five minutes after the Turkish surrender. The Turkish gunners look on (left of photograph) at the loss of their weapon.*

CENTER RIGHT: *Fighting carried on to the end in certain sectors. Here British armored cars are shelled by Turkish guns.*

BELOW: *The shallow draft to this British river boat can be appreciated in this photograph. The boat's guns blast away at Turkish positions along the Tigris.*

BELOW RIGHT: *Bulgarian troops man the fire-step of a well-dug trench on the Macedonian Front.*

Marshall's forces had completely outnumbered the dispirited Turks and after the fall of Mosul the Turks had no option but to seek terms with the British. Of all the campaigns fought by the British, the Mesopotamian adventure was the least productive. By the end of the campaign Marshall's forces – albeit widely dispersed – numbered hundreds of thousands, and the total number of troops employed in this theater between 1914-18 was 889,702 men. The only truly significant result of the campaign was that it tied down a relatively small number of Turks and facilitated Allenby's advance from Damascus. When the vast numbers of troops sucked into 'Mespot' are set against the desperate shortages of soldiers on the Western Front in 1918, the whole business resembled an almost criminal waste of resources and lives.

The Turks had fought resolutely against the British until the end, but the constant pressure of the campaigns in Palestine and Mesopotamia combined with the Allied blockade was too much for them. Furthermore, the collapse of Bulgaria at the end of September 1918 exposed Constantinople (present-day Istanbul) to an Allied advance from Salonika, forcing Turkey to sue for peace. Turkish representatives met those of the Allies and on 30 October 1918 the Armistice of Mudros was signed, thereby ending hostilities.

The Allied forces in Salonika made a surprising re-emergence in the autumn of 1918. The universally unpopular French Commander in Chief, General Maurice Sarrail, had gone and in July 1918 the dynamic General Franchet d'Esperey took command of a force comprising French, British, Italians, Serbs and Greeks. He immediately began planning a major offensive into occupied-

Serbia and Bulgaria. Although the Bulgarians had fought hard on the defensive along the border regions, by the summer of 1918 war-weariness was seriously undermining their morale and German aid was no longer forthcoming. Franchet d'Esperey launched his final attack on 1 September. The Serbs enthusiastically forced their way over the mountain passes of Macedonia into their homeland. Bulgarian resistance collapsed under the combined thrusts of French, Serbian and British forces and on 29 September an armistice was signed. This enabled the Allies to threaten Turkey and advance northward against the Austro-German armies in both Rumania and Hungary in October.

By 1918 Austria-Hungary's position was hopeless: politically, the increasing momentum of Slav nationalism was tearing the empire apart, while on the military side German aid had practically ceased. On the Italian front, however, the Austrian Army remained a fairly effective force. In June it launched its last offensive, a desperate attempt which was easily held by the Italian Army under the leadership of General Armando Diaz. The Italian Army had been substantially reorganized in the year since the Caporetto debacle and on 24 October it went over to the offensive. The Austrian defenses along the River Piave were breached and the Austrian Army began a general retreat. The Italians followed (with French and British support) and won the final victory at Vittorio Veneto. On 27 October the Austrians sued for peace and on 3 November an armistice brought the war on the Italian Front to an end. This, in effect, signaled the collapse of the Austro-Hungarian Empire.

Germany's end was not long delayed. The peace for which the High Command had clamored when the Hindenburg Line was broken proved hard to obtain. Instead, there followed a month of continuous defeat and retreat in

LEFT: Italian troops march down a mountain road in the Val d'Assa, 1918.

FAR LEFT, ABOVE: Italian infantrymen take up positions along the bank of the Piave River.

FAR LEFT, CENTER: Uniformed and equipped by France, a battalion of Serbian troops takes a break during an advance toward the Balkan Front.

BELOW LEFT: Men of the Serbian 2nd Infantry Regiment march through the town of Skopje on the way to liberate their homeland from the Austro-Hungarian yoke.

RIGHT: The collapse of the German Army on the Western Front, September–November 1918.

BELOW: Sure in the knowledge of victory, Italian soldiers pursue the enemy back to their Austrian homeland during the last few weeks of war.

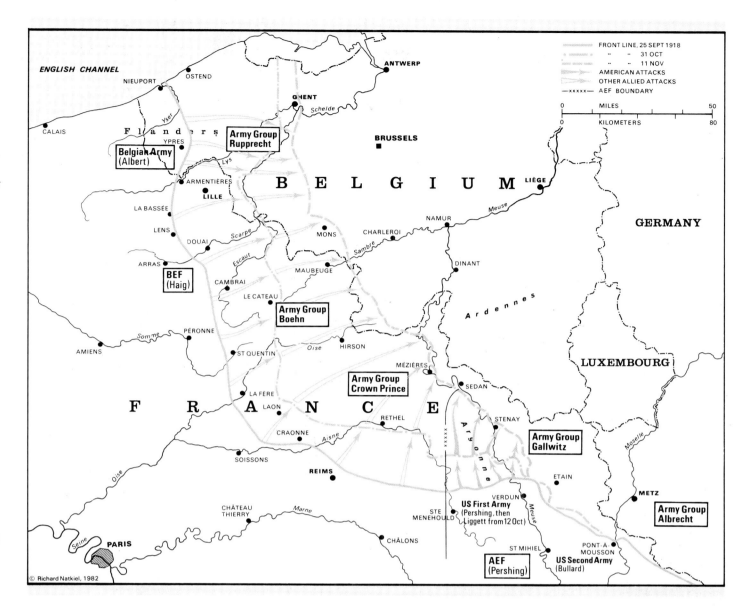

ABOVE LEFT: *Soldiers of a Scottish Canadian regiment move up to the start line for the Second Battle of Cambrai, October 1918. Wire-cutters are fitted to the muzzles of their rifles. The large number of Scottish immigrants in Canada led to the development of kilted units with avowedly Scottish connections.*

ABOVE: *Already veterans of the conflict, US troops of the 7th Division cheer the news of the Armistice, 11 November 1918.*

FAR LEFT: *The dejection of defeat; continuously on the retreat, an exhausted German infantry unit rests on the road during the final days of the war.*

LEFT: *No longer mighty conquerors, the German Army quietly slips out of Belgium, November 1918 – a far cry from the 'glorious' invasion of August 1914.*

RIGHT: *A few of the 188,700 German prisoners captured by the British Army during 1918. An indication of how decisive the British contribution was to the defeat of the German Army.*

ABOVE: Austrian troops take over a forward defensive line along the Trentino shortly before the final collapse. Despite their numerous disasters on the Eastern Front, the soldiers of the Austro-Hungarian Empire generally fought well in the Italian theater.

the West; the condition of the Army became steadily more critical. On 26 October Ludendorff was dismissed and replaced by General Wilhelm Gröner. Unrest was spreading through Germany with demands for the Kaiser's abdication. On 29 October mutiny broke out in the High Seas Fleet and by 4 November Kiel had become a revolutionary center with ships flying the red flag. With the German Army now scarcely able to fight and quite unable to move, the Allies launched their last offensive – the Americans ·again attacking in the Argonne; the British on the Sambre. Between them the two Allied Armies succeeded in taking 20,000 prisoners and 450 guns.

Revolution continued to spread through Germany and peace was now essential. On 7 November an armistice delegation crossed the lines. Two days later the Kaiser abdicated and fled to Holland. A republic was proclaimed with the Social Democrat Friedrich Ebert as Chancellor. Imperial Germany was in ruins, but the generals of the Imperial Army had an alibi for their defeat – the legendary 'stab in the back.' Yet the defeat was real enough; in the final three months of the war the Allies had taken 385,400 prisoners and 6615 guns, of which the British share was

just under 50 percent of the former and 40 percent of the latter. The great catastrophe ended at 1100 hours on 11 November when the armistice signed in Foch's specially fitted train took effect. The guns fell silent all along the line of conflict.

So ended the greatest war in human history to date. For the first time mass armies had fought each other armed with weapons provided by the industrial revolution. These technologies of mass destruction were an underlying cause of the war's enormous casualty lists. Accurate figures for total and individual national losses are extremely hard to come by, but can be reasonably estimated at a total of almost 13 million military deaths. These were succeeded by a far larger total of civilian deaths caused by an outbreak of influenza which spread through Europe in 1918-19, its deadly effect increased by the exhaustion of the European population following the rigors of the war.

Only on a national basis can the Western Allies' figures of casualties be considered accurate. Britain and its Empire suffered a total of 947,023 men killed, 2,121,906 wounded and 191,652 men taken prisoner. French victims amounted to 1,375,000 killed or missing, over 4,000,000 wounded and around 500,000 men taken prisoner. Italy's dead numbered about 460,000, with 947,000 wounded and 530,000 captured. The United States of America lost 115,600 (including those who died of disease in the USA), with 205,690 wounded and 4570 taken prisoner. Russia's figures are far from complete: 1,700,000 killed, 4,950,000 wounded and 2,500,000 imprisoned (many of whom died in captivity). Germany suffered 1,808,545 killed, 4,247,143 wounded and 1,152,000 taken prisoner (although official figures only allow for 617,922). Austro-Hungarian figures must remain largely conjectural but possibly number 1,200,000 dead, 3,620,000 wounded and 2,200,000 taken prisoner. Turkish figures are also estimated and remain incomplete: 325,000 killed, 400,000 wounded and a further 1,565,000 casualties 'untabulated.'

In the light of the massive national effort made by the Western Allies to secure victory, it was hardly surprising that they should seek to impose harsh terms on the

Collapse of the Home Front

The relentless stranglehold of the Allied blockade and the knowledge that the German Army was slowly disintegrating in the field caused despair among the German population. In a letter of 7 October 1918, Prince von Bulow, a prewar German Chancellor, bemoaned his compatriots' lack of national fervor during the last days of the war:

Would to God I had never lived to see this day! Why could I not have died while Germany was still in her greatness? . . . What hurts me most is this apathy and discouragement on all

sides and, with them, every sign of panic. Have things really got to such a point that we must lose our heads altogether? Did not the French go on fighting desperately, enduring defeat after defeat, at a time when we were already threatening Paris? Have our enemies reached the left bank of the Rhine? Are they in Alsace-Lorraine – in Baden? Are Aix-la-Chapelle, Coblenz, Freiburg or Mannheim in ruins? Is Cologne cathedral being shelled? It would need all this to place us in a similar situation to that in which the French have gone on fighting us for four years.

ABOVE: *The end for Wilhelmine Germany, November 1918 – German sailors refuse to accept their officers' orders to undertake a last, suicide mission against the Royal Navy. The refusal quickly grew into mutiny and then a full-scale revolution. Here, German sailors listen to demands put forward by a revolutionary representative of the armed forces.*

RIGHT: *Throughout the last week of the war Germany was in turmoil. The war was obviously lost – as was any credibility of the old order – and change was in the air. Political developments were followed avidly by the German people and vast crowds gathered for the declaration of Germany as a republic on 9 November.*

The Armistice

World War I was timed to end on the eleventh hour of the eleventh day of the eleventh month of 1918. At 1100 hours the fighting stopped (although there were a few cases where gunfire carried over the hour) and Europe found itself at peace after nearly 52 months of war. The reaction to the news varied from nation to nation and, most especially, between the soldiers and the civilians. The two following extracts illustrate the very different meaning the Armistice had for these two sections of the population:

Suddenly maroons went off, a startling explosion just above us. An air raid, an air raid! A woman ran out of a house and gazed anxiously at the sky. But before one could recollect that it might mean the Armistice, people were pouring out of buildings, streaming into the streets. The war was ended. Tools must have been downed in no time. Crowds grew bigger every minute.

There was great liveliness, calls, cries, whistles and hooters sounding, noise and crowds grew as we proceeded. Chancery Lane was very lively. Going out for lunch about one o'clock, great excitement prevailed; happy, daylight mafficking produced most unusual sights. Every vehicle going along the Strand was being boarded by people, most of whom waved flags. Boys and girls flung themselves on anywhere and clung as best they might. One scene was more unusual than others. At the corner of Chancery Lane a stout policeman on point duty was surrounded by girls all clamoring to dance with him. The London bobby rose to the occasion – without a word he took on one after another for a turn round on the narrow pavement as they stood, while his countenance remained absolutely impassive. Custom and convention melted away as if a new world had indeed dawned. Officers and privates mixed in equal comradeship. Privates drilled officers, munitionettes commanded platoons made up of both. The spirit of militarism was turned into comedy.

CAROLINE E PLAYNE.

On 11th November we marched back 15 miles to Bethencourt. A blanket of fog covered the countryside. At 11 o'clock we slung on our packs and tramped on along the muddy *pavé*. The band played, but there was very little singing. 'Before a man comes to be wise, he is half dead with catarrhes and aches, with sore eyes and a worn-out body.' We were very old, very tired and now very wise. We took over our billets and listlessly devoured a meal. In an effort to cure our apathy, the little American doctor from Vermont who had joined us a fortnight earlier broke his invincible teetotalism, drank half a bottle of whiskey, and danced a *cachucha*. We looked at his antics with dull eyes and at last put him to bed.

CAPTAIN GUY CHAPMAN, Royal Fusiliers.

defeated Central Powers, especially Germany, the country most responsible for the outbreak of war in 1914 and whose own war aims for both West and East were draconian in the extreme. Alsace and Lorraine were returned to France (taken by Germany in the 1870-71 Franco-Prussian War); the newly formed state of Poland was given a 'corridor' to the Baltic through Prussia; Germany's Air Force was abolished, her Navy denied U-boats and capital ships, and her Army reduced to 100,000 men. In addition a huge demand for reparations was made on a bankrupt Germany in order to help defray the cost of the war for the Allies (although the money was never paid). Lastly, a clause was inserted in the Treaty of Versailles stating that Germany was to be made 'responsible' for the war. In the face of overwhelming Allied military superiority, the German deputation reluctantly signed the treaty on 28 June 1919.

The old empire of Austria-Hungary was completely dismantled, bringing into existence the new states of Yugoslavia (Serb-dominated), Czechoslovakia and Poland. Russia remained a 'problem' as civil war had broken out between Red and White forces, the latter receiving military support from the Western Allies. Finland achieved full independence as did the Baltic states of Lithuania, Latvia and Estonia – at the expense of Russia.

The period 1918-21 was characterized by turmoil and upheaval as Europe readjusted to a new order. The three great empires of Germany, Austria-Hungary and Russia had gone for ever and the map of Central Europe had been redrawn to create a number of new states. By the early 1920s Europe had established some sort of new political order but the Versailles Treaty was not to remain a permanent settlement. Germany had suffered humiliation but was not comprehensively beaten. The Nazi rise to power in 1933 signaled the resumption of the great power struggle for the dominance in Europe. Tragically, World War I had failed to settle the issue; it was simply the first round in a conflict which would again erupt in open warfare in 1939. World War II decided the struggle for good but, paradoxically, the victors would be the great non-European continental superpowers of the Soviet Union and the United States of America.

LEFT: *The Armistice did not end violence in Germany as right and leftwing groups fought for control of the streets. The large numbers of available weapons and ex-soldiers ensured that political clashes would be bloody and the scene in this photograph is typical – a heavily armed truck, manned by militant leftwingers, drives through the center of Berlin.*

RIGHT: *Orpen's painting of the German delegate (back to viewer) signing the Treaty of Versailles captures the essential nature of the treaty: an imposition of terms by the victor on the vanquished. The leading Allied delegates (in the center: Wilson, Clemenceau and Lloyd George) look on, sure in the knowledge that justice had been done. This was not the German view, however.*